THE SAF

THE SAFFRON ROBE

A Life of Sadhu Sundar Singh

by

Janet Lynch-Watson

HODDER AND STOUGHTON
LONDON SYDNEY AUCKLAND TORONTO

 Printed in Great Britain for Hodder and Stoughton Limited, St. Paul's House, Warwick Lane, London EC4P 4AH by Cox & Wyman Ltd., London, Reading and Fakenham

To my husband

Acknowledgments

I WOULD LIKE to thank all those whose help and encouragement have made this book possible.

In particular, I am deeply grateful to the Right Reverend A. J. Appasamy, formerly Bishop in Coimbatore for his permission to use material from his book, *Sundar Singh, A Biography* (Lutterworth Press, 1958).

Others who have given me particular assistance include Miss Jean M. Woods, Librarian of the Church Missionary Society Library; the Reverend Richard Haigh, formerly a Church Missionary Society priest in North India; Miss Naomi Howell of the New Zealand Presbyterian Church's Committee on Mission Overseas; the Reverend D. M. Riddle of Auckland, New Zealand; and Miss Marina Chavchavadze.

I am further indebted to the authors of the following books: *The Gospel of Sundar Singh* by Friedrich Heiler (George Allen & Unwin Ltd.); *Sadhu Sundar Singh, Called of God* by Mrs Arthur Parker (Christian Literature Society for India); *Sadhu Sundar Singh* by C. F. Andrews (Hodder & Stoughton Ltd.); *The Sadhu* by B. H. Streeter and A. J. Appasamy (Macmillan & Co. Ltd.); *The Vision and the Call* by T. E. Riddle (Literature Committee of the Punjab Synod); *Apostle of the Bleeding Feet* by Alfred Zahir (C.M.S. Mission Press, Agra); *An Introduction to Indian Christian Theology* by Robin Boyd (The Christian Literature Society, Madras); *South* by Ernest Shackleton (William Heinemann Ltd.); *The Great Divorce* by C. S. Lewis (Geoffrey Bles Ltd.); *The Life of the Spirit and the Life Today* by Evelyn Underhill (Methuen & Co. Ltd.); *For Faith and Freedom* by Leonard Hodgson (Oxford

University Press); *Reality and Religion* by Sundar Singh (Macmillan & Co. Ltd.); *Visions of the Spiritual World* by Sundar Singh (Macmillan & Co. Ltd.); *With and Without Christ* by Sundar Singh (Cassell & Co. Ltd.).

Does the road wind uphill all the way?
Yes, to the very end

CHRISTINA GEORGINA ROSSETTI

1

MYSTIC LOST IN TIBET

Christian Preacher Who Visited London

FEARED VENGEANCE BY LAMAS?

FROM OUR OWN CORRESPONDENT, CALCUTTA.

Misgivings are felt among his followers in India regarding the safety of Sadhu Sundar Singh, the Christian mystic and preacher. Not a word has been heard of him since he entered Tibet in April on one of his preaching tours.

Morning Post, 18 November 1929

NEWSPAPERS ALL OVER the world, from Australia to Sweden, from Japan to America, reported the news that Sadhu Sundar Singh was missing.

He had failed to return from his last perilous visit to Tibet. People searched, prayed and hoped but he was never seen again.

Mystery and uncertainty surround the circumstances of his disappearance. One thing that is certain is the profound influence this remarkable Indian had on people of many races across the world.

His story begins on 3rd September 1889. He was born the youngest son of a rich Sikh landowner and farmer called Sardar Sher Singh. The family lived at Rampur in the State of Patiala, a village set in the dusty Punjab plain in the north of India.

Sundar's father, being an elder brother, was the head of the whole family. He was a man of authority and greatly esteemed in Rampur as a local leader. Sundar with his brothers, sisters and cousins would have lacked nothing in the material sense. It was a secure home for a child to grow up in. The days followed a steady, ordered pattern, broken only by regular visits to the Himalayas each summer. They often stayed at Simla where the cool mountain climate was a welcome relief after the heat of the plains.

Their family life was strong, rooted in a dignified Sikh heritage. They traced their faith back to the sixteenth century when the founder Guru Nanak sought to blend the best of Hinduism and Mohammedanism. Their creed can be summed up simply as a belief in the fatherhood of God and the brotherhood of man.

Thus Sundar's Sikh faith with its emphasis on a personal God and its rejection of the Hindu caste system, prepared the ground for his later Christian conviction. Christianity was not a rejection of his ancestral beliefs but a fulfilment of them.

For Sundar in his childhood years the dominant feature of his life was the love between him and his mother who was no less esteemed than her husband. Women are given a place of honour in Sikh families and she was especially revered for her deep religious belief.

So far she had failed to kindle this same spark of devotion in her elder sons, but with Sundar, her youngest boy, she had a particular, tender affinity.

From an early age he accompanied her to Hindu temples; he walked proudly beside her when she went to consult the Sikh 'sadhu' or holy man.

His mother was remarkably liberal in her religious attitudes.

She did not despise the beliefs of others for she felt truth was clothed in many forms. Through her Sundar received a grounding not only in the religious writings of the Sikhs, but was also introduced to the holy books of the Hindus and the Moslems.

Sundar's mother used to say to him, "You must not be careless and worldly like your brothers. You must seek peace of soul and love religion and some day you must become a holy sadhu."

"You must seek peace of soul"—thus she started her son on his quest for peace, a search that was to dominate his childhood and adolescence and drive him to the depths of suicidal despair before he found what he was seeking.

In Sundar's own writings we see glimpses of his early years.

A small boy, five years old, wakes one morning and calls to his mother, "I'm hungry. Can I get my milk?"

"No, Sundar," his mother chides, "your prayers first, food later."

This was a scene that was often repeated. No doubt Sundar rebelled, and sometimes he was punished, but in later years he was to remember his mother with gratitude for this early discipline.

"Although at that time," he wrote in one of his books, "I was too young to appreciate the value of these things, yet later on I realised their value, and now, whenever I think of it, I thank God for that training, and I can never be sufficiently thankful to God for giving me such a mother, who in my earliest years instilled in me the love and fear of God."

It was during these early morning devotions that he would have learnt by heart the Bhagavad Gita, part of the Hindu scriptures in Sanskrit. It was a considerable undertaking for a seven-year-old.

At the time of his seventh birthday Sundar and his mother set out from Rampur across the plain to the jungle country.

It was hot, it was dusty, but Sundar did not notice. Today he was to recite part of the Bhagavad Gita to the holy man in the jungle. It was not the first time he had made the journey. Often he trotted along with his mother on her regular visits.

The shade of the trees was welcoming after the burning sun. Soon Sundar and his mother were standing before the sadhu. Sundar, his brown eyes bright, could hardly wait to begin his recitation.

The sadhu was pleased with him, and Sundar listened with pride as the old man and his mother discussed how he might grow up to be a holy man, devoting his life to God.

His father was less pleased. Much as he respected his wife, he felt that such behaviour in a boy so young was unnatural. Night after night he found his son reading the holy scriptures.

"It is bad for your health to read so late," he said. "Listen, Sundar, boys of your age think of nothing but games and play, but why has this mania possessed you at so early an age?"

Sundar may have been tempted as the years passed to take his father's advice. Despite his reading, despite his prayers, despite the teaching in meditation and yoga that he received from holy men, Sundar had not found the peace he was seeking. However, encouraged by his mother he did not give up.

On one occasion his father sent him off with pocket money to spend at the bazaar. While thinking what he would buy, Sundar met an old woman, cold and hungry. He was so moved at her plight that he handed her the money and ran quickly back to his father.

"There is an old woman, Father, whom I found near the bazaar very cold and without food. We must help her. Can I give her a blanket?" To his horror his father refused. "I have already helped her many times. Let someone else take their turn." Sundar was amazed and angry. How could his father be so callous? In a moment of rebellion he took five rupees out of his father's pocket intending to buy a blanket the next day.

"Sundar, I have lost some money. Do you know where it is?" his father asked him that evening. "No, Father," came the reply.

That night Sundar could not sleep. He was a thief and a liar. By the time morning came he knew he would have to tell his father what he had done. As he summoned up his courage he wondered how he would be punished.

But his father did not punish him. He put his arm round his young son. "I have always trusted you, Sundar, and now I have good proof that I was not wrong. Buy the blanket and buy yourself some sweets with this," and he gave Sundar another rupee.

Sundar went to the American Presbyterian Mission School in Rampur. The government school which he could have attended was three miles away, so it seemed sensible to spare him the journey and let him receive his education locally.

Here for the first time Sundar encountered the Bible, which was taught every day. He was furious. To think that he, a Sikh, should be forced to read and study the book of the despised Christians. He remembered the proud history of the Sikh religion. His was a faith that men had fought and died for. It was not for nothing that he bore the name of 'Singh', a title meaning 'lion' and used by the Sikhs since the early eighteenth century. Sundar openly defied his Christian teachers and led other boys to do the same. He was a precocious child and used his knowledge of Hindu scripture and of the Granth, which is the Sikh holy book, to counter the arguments of the missionaries.

With the help of his mother's influence, Sundar might have outgrown his rebelliousness and come to regard the Christian school with a greater sense of perspective, for his mother had been friendly with some of the women of the Christian mission and would surely have helped him to a more moderate attitude.

But Sundar's mother died. He was fourteen at the time. Suddenly his world disintegrated. His love for his mother and their deep understanding of each other had been the cornerstone of his life. Only she had understood his search for spiritual peace. Without her his chances of finding it seemed ever less likely. His mother's death left him with a sense of desolation and anger, and his elder brother's death shortly afterwards confirmed his mood.

He directed the bitterness of his heart towards the Christians at the mission school. "Please let me leave the Christian school," he pleaded to his father. Sardar Sher Singh, downcast by his wife's death, was in no mood to argue. Sundar changed schools. For three months Sundar made the hot and dusty journey across the plain to the government school. Persecuting and annoying the local Christian community was now confined to out-of-school hours but Sundar and his friends took every opportunity. People who had known the gentle child who went with his mother to the temple were amazed and saddened at the change.

As the summer progressed Sundar found the daily trek to school more and more wearisome, until at last it was obvious his health was not going to survive the strain of walking six miles a day in the Indian sun. Hesitantly his father approached the mission school again and they agreed to take his son back, although they must have felt some reluctance.

A tight-lipped, sullen boy returned to the Christians. They longed to help him for his unhappiness was plain to see. Yet he resolutely refused their friendship or the comfort of their faith. His manner, although less aggressive, was still resentful.

Occasionally he did look at a copy of the New Testament which they had given him, but what his own religious books had failed to provide he did not expect to find in the Christians' book. Yet one phrase leapt out of the page at him, "Come unto me, all ye that labour and are heavy laden, and I will give you rest." Could that be the answer? He thought not and he continued to show his contempt of Christianity.

This contempt was such that one day when the shadow of a missionary passed across him, Sundar set about washing himself to obliterate the stain, making great display of his action.

His father observed his behaviour sadly, unable to understand his confused and unhappy son. One day in December 1904 Sher Singh, hearing shouting and laughter coming from the courtyard of his house in Rampur, went out to investigate. There was his son, surrounded by a cheering group of young friends, tearing up a copy of the New Testament, and throwing the pages on to a bonfire. He walked across to Sundar and remonstrated with him.

"Don't be a fool, Sundar. That is the Christians' book, and a good book. What has got into you, that you do such evil things?" Sundar did not know what had got into him. Indeed he almost envied his brothers and friends who appeared satisfied with life as it was. Such satisfaction eluded him. There remained this emptiness, this nagging thirst for God. To whomsoever he turned, the advice was the same.

"Wait until you are older, Sundar, and you will come to understand these things." Sundar grew weary of waiting. "Why should I have to wait?" Sundar asked himself with all the impatience of a young man. What could he do to bring the matter to a head? How could he force the issue?

Three days after the incident of the burned New Testament Sundar decided what to do. At three o'clock in the morning he rose from his bed. It was dark and very quiet. Occasionally the calls of a wild animal broke the stillness of the Indian night.

Sundar doused himself with cold water to shake off the effects of sleep. Then he began a vigil of prayer. He prayed that if there was a God, that he should reveal himself. Sundar made up his mind that if he did not find the peace he was seeking, he would commit suicide.

At five o'clock that morning the Ludhiana express train was due to pass close by their house. Sundar determined that if his prayers remained unanswered he would lie down on the track in the path of the train.

As the minutes passed Sundar knelt and prayed fervently. When only half an hour remained he was disturbed by the orange glow of a light shining in his room. Thinking perhaps it came from another part of the house, he cautiously opened the door but all was dark and silent. He turned back into his room half expecting the light to have vanished. But still it remained, growing steadily brighter moment by moment.

Describing this awesome experience in later years, Sundar wrote, "The light increased in intensity and took the form of a globe of light above the ground. In this light there appeared, not the form I expected but the Living Christ whom I had counted dead." Had the revelation been of Krishna or even Buddha, Sundar might not have been so overwhelmed. But there before him was the form of Jesus of Nazareth whom he had despised and rejected.

Jesus spoke to him in Hindustani, "*Tu mujhe kyun satata hai? Dekh main ne tere liye apui jan salib par di.*"—"Why do you persecute me? Remember I gave my life for you upon the cross." Then Sundar recognised the scars of the Crucified Jesus and it was this sight that brought him to his knees in adoration.

At this moment there was one dominant thought in his mind, "This Jesus is alive—not dead and buried as I had supposed." Moreover there was love for him in those eyes and the promise of forgiveness, forgiveness even for one who had burned the Bible.

Sundar said afterwards, "My heart was filled with inexpressible joy and peace, and my whole life was entirely changed." The peace that indwelt him at that moment was like a steady flame never to be extinguished.

Like Saint Paul he had been confronted with the Risen Christ even while persecuting his followers. Throughout his life Sundar was to experience times of ecstasy and elation while in communion with God in prayer. In such states he had visions of heaven and met people he knew to be dead. Yet he was convinced that this first vision of Christ, when he was fifteen years old, was distinct and different in kind from any that were to follow. He always insisted that it was an objective occurrence, quite external to himself, and totally unexpected since he believed Jesus Christ to be dead. He said once, "I have had visions and I know how to distinguish them, but Jesus I have only seen once." He preferred to describe the events of this night as an 'appearance' of Jesus rather than a 'vision' of Jesus.

The events of the night of 17th December 1904 defy analysis. Controversial arguments concerning the authenticity of the 'appearance' have been proposed and countered. Similarities to Saul's encounter on the Damascus Road are obvious, and Sundar would have heard the story in the Acts of the Apostles read at school. It has been argued that with Paul's experience in the back of his mind, Sundar's strained nervous state and colourful imagination took care of the rest.

Other commentators have been discomfited by an alleged element of spiritual blackmail. After all, Sundar did appear to dictate terms and, so to speak, put God under duress.

In considering all this we must keep it within the Indian context and perspective. For Indians of Sundar's generation the reality of the spiritual world impinged upon them daily. To our materialistic Western understanding half a century later, all this is unfamiliar ground. We can so easily forget that Sundar's experience would not have been deemed unusual by his contemporaries.

What remains after the dust of the arguments has settled is the incontrovertible evidence of a changed life. 'You will recognise them by the fruits they bear. Can grapes be picked from briars, or figs from thistles? In the same way a good tree always yields good fruit, and a poor tree bad fruit.' (St Matthew, 7 : 16–17, NEB). Surely the acid test of the genuineness of mystical experience is the effect it has on the subject's subsequent life?

In Sundar's case we note that the ensuing sense of inward peace transformed the quality of his whole personality and was never to leave him. From henceforth his life had one overriding purpose, to follow in the steps of the Risen Lord, who had been so wondrously revealed to him.

As day dawned on 18th December 1904 Sundar's search ended. As he knelt on the bedroom floor of his home in Rampur the glorious light faded, but God was found.

2

THE LUDHIANA EXPRESS thundered past. Full of joy, Sundar rose from his knees.

"Father, Father, wake up! I must talk to you." Sundar rushed into his father's room and roused him. "Listen, Father. I have seen Jesus Christ. He is alive." Sher Singh turned over sleepily. What was the boy saying?

"I have seen Jesus, Father. I am a Christian."

Sundar's father sat up. "What are you talking about? It is only three days since you burned their book. You're over-excited. Go back to bed." Sher Singh lay down again and closed his eyes. The boy must have been dreaming.

"It was just a dream, Sundar," said one of the family the next day when he tried to explain.

"You have been reading too late at night. We've always said you shouldn't. You ought to rest a bit more. You will make yourself ill, Sundar, if you go on like this."

"You are a Sikh, Sundar. Are you mad, believing what those Christians at the school tell you?" So his family persuaded and reasoned.

"I am now a Christian," Sundar insisted again and again. To his family it now became apparent that Sundar meant what he said. The shame and disgrace of it, that one of their family, a family respected for miles around, should turn his back on the faith of his fathers and take up with these Christians. Christianity wasn't for Indians. It was the Europeans' religion. How could Sundar be so disloyal?

The tide of their anger swept against Sundar but he held his ground. It was not easy to endure the reproaches, the stunned disappointment of his father, the bitter anger of his brother.

The hostility would have been easier to bear had Sundar not cared so deeply for his family and its Sikh traditions.

Sundar became the talk of Rampur. The situation became even more acute when three other Sikh boys, fellow-pupils with Sundar at the American Presbyterian Mission School, joined him in saying they wished to receive Christian Baptism. Strong and immediate parental opposition brought two of them to heel, yet the resentment of the village against the school grew daily in fervour.

The Headmaster, the Reverend E. P. Newton, was brought before the local magistrate and accused of putting undue pressure on his pupils. Sundar testified in his Headmaster's defence. "My decision to become a Christian was mine alone. I have received a direct revelation of Jesus the Lord."

It was a hard lonely time for Sundar Singh. Still only fifteen years old he had to face the hostility both of his family and the local community. In addition by embracing the Christian faith he felt he had brought about the rampant anti-Christian spirit in the village. Indeed the hue and cry which followed upon Sundar's conversion forced the school to close and many Christians left the district.

Gurdit Singh, the other Sikh boy who had become a Christian, had been baptised at Khanna, a mission centre about two hundred miles along the railway line towards Ludhiana. Gurdit's father went to Khanna and persuaded his son to return to Rampur by telling the boy that his mother was ill. Soon after he reached home, Gurdit became very sick and died. His family rather than bear the disgrace of a Christian in the family had apparently poisoned his food. When news of this tragedy reached Sundar he was made to realise afresh how intense Sikh feelings were against his new faith.

Although his school had been forced to close down, its

former Headmaster, Mr Newton, continued to befriend Sundar. He was anxious to ensure that Sundar should continue his education in a Christian school. Fortunately there was a Christian Boys' Boarding School at Ludhiana and arrangements were made for Sundar to become a boarder there. No doubt Sher Singh was not altogether sorry to see his son leave Rampur for a while even though the school's Christian tradition would have displeased him.

The Presbyterian missionary teachers, Dr Wherry and Dr Fife welcomed Sundar warmly. Yet despite the friendliness with which he was received, Sundar nonetheless felt ill at ease in this new and unfamiliar environment. The staff were largely English-speaking and Sundar knew little English. His recent experiences and his thoughtful, introspective disposition tended to isolate him from the other boys. Worst of all he was deeply aggrieved to see how casually some of them appeared to regard their Christian faith. Within weeks Sundar made the decision to return home in the hope that the turmoil in Rampur had quietened in his absence.

Initially the welcome he received in Rampur was encouraging.

"Sundar has come home. Doubtless he's come to his senses at last!" they thought. These expectations were short-lived, for Sundar's return had not been occasioned by any renunciation of the Christian faith. On the contrary his Christian resolve had never been stronger. The cajoling and threatening began once more.

Behind the scenes his family worked on a new ploy. An uncle, a man of considerable wealth, invited Sundar to his home. On arrival he took Sundar down to the cellar and locked the door behind them. Sundar, somewhat alarmed, recalled the fate of his friend Gurdit Singh. Had his own family a similar murderous intent?

He eyed his uncle apprehensively as he moved towards a heavy iron safe. He opened the door to reveal a profusion of money and jewellery. His uncle smiled kindly and said, "You may have all this, Sundar, on condition you remain within the religion of your fathers."

Sundar could not help but be flattered by his uncle's generosity and by the depth of feeling that prompted it.

"No, uncle, I cannot," he said softly. "You must allow me to follow the truth as I see it."

As we have seen it was not only his family but also the wider community of the village who took strong exception to his new found faith. Households in the village ostracised him. His mother had been locally revered as a 'bhakta', that is, someone who is acknowledged as having religious insight and perception of a high order. This made her son's behaviour appear even more incomprehensible in the eyes of the people. When Sundar walked down the street backs were turned and fists shaken in his face: nonconformity then, as ever, roused fear and suspicion.

One local character, Rahmat Ullah, appears to have been notably aggressive. The incident is recounted of how he found Sundar early one evening seated in the shade of a tree, engrossed in his New Testament. Rahmat leant over him, his eyes wild and angry, snatched the New Testament and hurled it away.

"That's what I think of that," he blustered and cuffing Sundar he hurried away, anxious to tell his tale to Sundar's family.

A day or so later, Sundar came upon a crowd standing outside Rahmat's house. "Rahmat," he was told in hushed tones, "is critically ill and is dying of cholera."

On an impulse Sundar asked if he could see him, and was taken to Rahmat's bedside. The sick man looked at Sundar with wild staring eyes. He was in a weak and semi-delirious condition and spoke feverishly of devils who were coming to get him. "There is One who might save me but I dare not call him," he whispered.

"Who do you mean? Who is the One?" said Sundar.

"Your Guru," sobbed Rahmat and moments later he died.

Despite Sundar's intransigence the family did not slacken their efforts. What other inducement could they devise to get him to alter course?

A cousin, Spuran Singh, invited him to stay with him at Nabha, where Spuran Singh had an influential post in the service of the Maharaja. Although this was of course during the period of British rule in India the local princes or maharajas still had considerable power. Their loyalty to the Crown during the period of the Indian Mutiny had been rewarded by guarantees of territorial rights, and they now shared with the British the government of their states.

The Maharaja was therefore a much respected person, and Sundar was naturally alarmed when Spuran Singh told him that the Maharaja wished to see him. With all his authority, the Maharaja appealed to Sundar not to dishonour the Sikhs. He held out the offer of a promising career in his employ. Such a chance would have tempted any Sikh boy, but Sundar politely yet resolutely declined it.

It was now abundantly clear that Sundar Singh had a single-minded commitment to Christ. His family decided to play their last card.

"It is obvious to us Sundar that you are obsessed with your new-found faith. It seems you will sacrifice almost anything in pursuit of it. This we respect, but in the interests of your family who love you dearly will you make one concession?" Sundar had no desire needlessly to alienate them.

"What is it you want?"

"Keep your faith a secret, a private matter between your God and yourself."

Momentarily Sundar faltered. But no, to agree to this would be to strike at the heart of the Gospel. Sundar shook his head, "I am sorry, but I cannot agree to such a thing." From that time on he knew, and his family knew that he was lost to them. As a final gesture he took a pair of scissors and cut off his long black hair. As the Sikhs are bound by their religion to allow their hair to grow freely, Sundar's act was an outward and visible sign that he had turned his back on his old allegiance.

His father was incensed. "You cannot stay within my house a moment longer. You must leave tonight."

He was hungry. He was cold. He huddled for shelter under a tree on the outskirts of the village. He had nothing but the clothes he had been wearing and his copy of the New Testament. He thought of the home he had left, warm, comfortable and, until today, friendly. Now he was shivering, faint from lack of food and, worst of all, humanly speaking he was friendless. Yet he felt a great sense of peace that night, the peace born of a good conscience. It was he said later "my first night in heaven". A major battle had been fought and won. By God's good grace he had been enabled to stand firm for his Master.

When the morning light came he got to his feet and walked to the railway station at Rampur. The moment had come when he must leave behind him his home and village. The familiar houses, the dusty streets, the trees where he and his friends had played and gossiped, the Hindu temple which held the memories of his mother, all these belonged to earlier days. No more could he call them 'home'. A new life was beckoning to him although he perceived only dimly what its shape might be.

He hurried on leaving his childhood behind him. Sundar

Singh, tall and well-built for his age, had reached his manhood. He was not yet sixteen, but in India young men develop more rapidly than their European counterparts, and Sundar's particular experiences and determined character had wrought in him maturity and independence.

He reached the railway station. What now? Where? The Christians who had fled from Rampur at the time of Sundar's conversion were now settled at Rupar, a town one hundred and fifty miles to the north-west. Sundar knew they would welcome him. He had just sufficient money for his fare.

The train drew out of Rampur. Sundar sat back in his seat. He could no longer ignore a pain in his stomach that had been troubling him since early that morning. Sundar told himself it was cramp brought on by his cold uncomfortable night. Though he tried not to think of it, his mind kept recalling his friend Gurdit Singh and the fate he had suffered. As the pain intensified the thought of Gurdit's death clamoured for recognition. Had he driven his family to act in a similar way?

To Sundar the journey to Rupar seemed interminable. When at last the train pulled into Rupar station, he struggled out of the carriage and laboriously made his way to the home of the pastor, the Reverend P. C. Uppal and his wife. He reached the doorstep only just in time, collapsing minutes later in their living-room. The boy was obviously very ill and Mr Uppal called a doctor at once. Sundar was right in his suspicions. He had indeed been poisoned and was fortunate to have survived the journey.

"There is nothing I can do, Mr Uppal," the doctor told the pastor. "The boy will soon die, I fear. I will not give him any medicines, for there is no prospect of recovery, and his relatives will only complain that my medicines killed him. I will come back tomorrow morning and we will arrange the funeral."

Just before leaving the doctor looked in again at Sundar,

and found that he had regained consciousness. He bent down to hear what the boy said.

"Would you please read to me?" Sundar indicated the New Testament by the bed, "Saint Mark, Chapter Sixteen, please." It was the account of Christ's resurrection. The doctor read it to indulge his dying patient, but could not refrain from pointing out what a ridiculous story it seemed to him to be. He left expecting that Sundar would be dead by nightfall.

Sundar lay there, watched over by Mrs Uppal. Not for a moment did he believe he was going to die. Surely God still had work for him to do in this life? As his prayers upheld him through the night slowly his strength returned.

In the morning, a smiling Mrs Uppal helped him sit up in bed. By mid-day he had recovered sufficiently to sit outside in the afternoon sunshine.

As he rejoiced in his recovery Sundar caught sight of the doctor arriving. The doctor's face as he walked across to Sundar was a study in itself. The corpse he had expected was very much alive and smiling broadly. This incident had its sequel for, several years later, Sundar, on a preaching tour in Burma, met that same doctor again.

"Do you recognise me?" said the doctor.

"Yes," said Sundar, "the last time I met you I was at death's door." The doctor then told him that he had been astonished to see Sundar sitting up in the garden having made so miraculous a recovery. It had sent him back with renewed curiosity to the pages of the New Testament.

"I was baptised two years later," he told Sundar, "and I'm now working in Burma as a missionary doctor."

That doctor was the first of many for whom an encounter with Sundar Singh led to an encounter with Christ. Such was the quality of his life, the strength of his faith that people who met him were stopped in their tracks, made to think and often the whole direction of their lives was altered. Even as a young boy of fifteen, sick and helpless, there was something about his bearing and determination that spoke to the doctor.

When Sundar was fit enough to travel it was decided he should return to the boarding school at Ludhiana for the summer term. Sundar's longing was to be baptised, but he could not take this step without his father's permission until he was sixteen years old, and that would not be until 3rd September 1905.

His father, Sher Singh, discovered that Sundar was at Ludhiana, and he together with other members of the family arrived unexpectedly at the school intending to force Sundar to return with them.

Frustrated in their attempt to kill Sundar by poisoning, they approached the school in a spirit of angry determination.

Wisely the school authorities allowed only Sher Singh to see Sundar. The rest of the family were persuaded to leave the precincts and return home. It was a painful scene for between father and son lay the knowledge that there had been the abortive poison attempt. Once more his father pleaded with him to return. Past grievances would be forgotten if Sundar would relinquish Christianity.

Sundar had fought and overcome that particular temptation weeks ago and now even the sight of his father's tears could do nothing to change his mind. Disappointed, Sher Singh changed his tactics. He lost his temper and became abusive.

"You will not continue to disgrace your family and myself," he shouted. "We've failed once but we shall find a way to bring this nonsense to an end." With this veiled threat Sher Singh concluded the interview.

Doctor Fife, the Headmaster, was anxious to shield Sundar from further harassment by his family. Accordingly he recommended that Sundar should take refuge at Sabathu where the

American Presbyterian Mission that ran the Ludhiana school, also had a hospital for the treatment of lepers.

"I am very sorry to lose you Sundar but the risks will be less at Sabathu. If you remain there until you are sixteen then you can be baptised."

The tranquillity of the hospital at Sabathu was a welcome relief after those turbulent nine months since his conversion. Free from hostility and recrimination Sundar read and re-read his New Testament and prepared himself for baptism in the relaxed and gentle atmosphere of Sabathu. It became for him a symbol of quiet and rest, and when ill health prompted the need for a permanent base later in his life, it was in Sabathu that he bought a house.

Sabathu lies amongst the lower ranges of the Himalayas, a thousand feet below the town of Simla which held memories for him of childhood summer holidays. Sabathu is a beautiful town with wide views over the valleys across to wooded hills. Simla can be seen in the distance. Pine forests reach down to the boundaries of the Leper Hospital. The Punjab plains lie shimmering in the heat to the south and west, while in the opposite direction tower the majestic Himalayas, their snow-crowned peaks alluring yet daunting. Beyond them lay Tibet. Increasingly Sundar's thoughts were to turn in that direction.

Tibet was a mysterious land, closed to the world outside. Since the country had succumbed to Chinese rule at the end of the eighteenth century, foreigners had been unwelcome. It was a nation held together by its strong Buddhist faith and ruled by the Buddhist lamas, at that time notorious for their ignorance and cruelty. China's power and influence were temporarily to wane, but the policy of isolation persisted. The Tibetans had never forgotten the prophecy of a Buddhist saint who had foretold an invasion of their land and the consequent overthrow of their established religion. The lamas were therefore most anxious to keep all foreign influence at bay and were particularly fearful of Christianity and other alien faiths. The physical terrain of Tibet greatly aided them in their efforts to shut out the rest of the world. Only the most persevering visitors would be inclined to tackle the dangerous mountain routes and the bitter climate. Even that part of Tibet known as 'Lesser Tibet' or the 'Border of Tibet' and under British rule, was just as hostile to the outsider.

Sundar looked towards the mountain passes that led to that land and his heart went out to a people who had never so much as heard the name of Jesus Christ.

September approached and with it Sundar's sixteenth birthday. Arrangements were made for his baptism. Doctor Fife of the Ludhiana School wrote a letter of introduction to an Anglican priest, the Reverend J. Redman of the Church Missionary Society at Simla. He told him Sundar's story and of his deep yearning for baptism.

Happy that he was soon to be granted his greatest wish, Sundar eagerly made his way to Simla to meet Mr Redman and his wife. There was an immediate rapport between them. Their meeting marked the beginning of a longstanding friendship. For Sundar who had no settled home, it was reassuring to know that at the Redmans' a room was always ready for him. Mr Redman wrote later of their first meeting, "I was deeply impressed by his sincerity. I examined him carefully and asked him a great many questions about the chief facts of the Gospel. Sundar Singh replied to my entire satisfaction and he evinced even then an extraordinary knowledge of the life and teaching of Christ. Then I inquired into his personal experience of Christ as his Saviour. Again I was more than satisfied. And I told him I would be very glad to baptise him on the following day which was a Sunday."

Why it was that Sundar was baptised by a Church of England priest at Simla rather than by a minister of the American Presbyterian Mission at Sabathu is not entirely clear but was probably a matter of simple convenience. It seems likely that there was no resident minister at Sabathu and fortunately Mr Redman was near at hand.

At that time denominational distinctions meant little to Sundar, and this remained so for the rest of his life. More than perhaps any other Christian leader of his generation he demonstrated a faith which was free from sectarian preoccupations.

Thus on his sixteenth birthday, Sunday, 3rd September 1905, Sundar Singh was baptised at Saint Thomas's Church, Simla. The opening words of the Twenty-third Psalm used during his baptism were an apt commentary on both his past and his future:

"The Lord is my shepherd: therefore can I lack nothing."

3

SUNDAR WAS JUST sixteen. He had no money, no possessions. His relations were hostile, his friends few. No family eagerly planned his future, advising and encouraging him. It was a harsh beginning for any enterprise. Yet he was joyful and eager. Sundar knew what God had called him to do. The preliminaries were over. He had withstood many pressures, and he knew that he had only done so by the power of God working in him. The Lord had shepherded him through each rebuff, had strengthened him in temptation, and delivered him from certain death. Having publicly witnessed to his faith by receiving baptism, Sundar was eager to serve the God who had brought him thus far.

Thirty-three days after his baptism he left Sabathu. He was dressed in a plain robe of saffron cotton and a turban, both traditional garments of an Indian sadhu.

His mother's ambition for him was fulfilled. The little boy who had stood beside her under the trees and recited the Bhagavad Gita to the Hindu holy man, now gave his life to the service of God as a sadhu. That he did so as a Christian would not, he knew, have distressed his mother. She alone of his family would have understood his experience of Christ, and she alone would have recognised the compulsion of his vocation.

There is no doubt that her influence on him had been strong and her example and her wishes were as important as his new faith in setting him on his chosen road. He was later to say he had attended the best theological college in the world—his mother's bosom. Years later, in 1920, Sadhu Sundar Singh visited England and met the Archbishop of Canterbury, Doctor Randall Davidson. In their discussion Sundar spoke warmly of his mother's gentle upbringing, and how he learned from her the love of the Lord. "If I do not see my mother in heaven, I shall ask God to send me to hell so that I may be with her," he told the Archbishop.

To appreciate what Sundar Singh was trying to do as a Christian sadhu, it is necessary to understand the place of the 'sadhu' in the religious life of India. C. F. Andrews, a missionary of long experience in India, wrote, "India, perhaps more than any other country in the world, has felt in her soul this thirst for the living God. No one, who has watched the long line of pilgrims on their way to some sacred shrine, can ever forget the mystery of this heart-longing to seek and find God's presence." Many men in India devote their lives to this quest. Some, called 'sadhus', spend all their days in God's service. 'Sanyasis' on the other hand take up the life after a secular career. Both wear the yellow robe and have no settled home or money. They are dependent on others for food. There were many at that time whose lives were a credit to the sadhu-concept. But there were some who disgraced the ideal, or used it merely as an excuse to beg. Spectacular self-mortification, such as lying on a bed of nails or refusal to wash seem to Western minds unproductive exercises. Such practices though common were by no means universal amongst sadhus. Frequently the life of the sadhu expressed the highest and best in Hindu spirituality.

> Then he said to them: 'Go forth to every part of the world, and proclaim the Good News to the whole creation.' (St Mark 16 : 15 NEB).

> He said to them: 'The crop is heavy, but labourers are scarce; you must therefore beg the owner to send labourers to harvest his crop.

'Be on your way. And look, I am sending you like lambs among wolves. Carry no purse or pack, and travel barefoot. Exchange no greetings on the road.' (St Luke 10 : 2–4 NEB).

His mother's teaching in the Hindu and Sikh faiths on the one hand, and the words of Jesus Christ on the other—these two lines of thought converged like an arrow in Sundar Singh and set him on his way.

Jesus had told his followers to tell the good news to all the world. Sundar Singh obeyed. He followed the command quite simply, quite literally. He took no money, no shoes. He had two possessions, a blanket and his Urdu New Testament.

Since his first acquaintance with Christians, one thing in particular had troubled Sundar. They were so un-Indian. They wore Western clothes, they sang Western hymns; they brought not only the Christianity of the New Testament but also the whole paraphernalia of Western religious culture as well. Sundar Singh had been reared outside that culture. This enabled him to distinguish between the essential message of the New Testament (timeless and universal) and the 'packaging' (largely Victorian and European) in which it was being offered to the Indian people. Throughout his life Sundar sought to proclaim the Gospel with an authentic Indian accent and not in tones and cadences imported from abroad.

This was the predicament that faced and still faces the Indian Church, as indeed it does churches in Africa, China or New Guinea. Sundar Singh instinctively perceived the dilemma, and it was for this reason he did not join the missionaries at Sabathu, but set out on his own.

A story that Sundar often told illustrates his purpose. He was once on a train returning to north India from Bombay. At a stop along the line he saw through the window a Brahmin priest being helped by his friends out of the train, having been overwhelmed by the heat. The stationmaster hurried towards the fainting figure with a cup of water. The Brahmin though desperately in need, refused the water. According to the rules of his religion, he would pollute himself if he drank from anything but his own brass drinking vessel. "I will not break my caste," he said, "I am willing to die." One of his companions fetched his own cup. The water was poured into it and he drank gladly.

"It is the same with the Water of Life," explained Sundar. "Indians do need the Water of Life, but not in a European cup."

Thus it was that on 6th October 1905 a tall upright figure in a flowing saffron robe left Sabathu. His dark hair was hidden in a turban, similar to the one he had worn as a Sikh. He saw no reason to abandon his Indian form of dress in favour of a Western style. His beard grew freely; his eyes shone bright and dark against his pale brown complexion. He was a young man in his prime, compelling in his bearing and appearance. He went barefoot and without luggage. He would eat what he was given, but he would not beg. He would rest where he was offered shelter; if necessary he would sleep in the open.

He began his preaching tour in the country around Simla, going from village to village and delivering his message. It was hard going. Warm welcomes turned into bitter hostility when his listeners realised that it was the Christians' God he spoke of. His bare feet were often cut and scratched. This was mountain country and the nights were cold. A day's hard climbing from one village to another would end with doors being barred and a night spent shivering and hungry in the open. It was a great contrast to the life he had known as a boy. All this time Sundar knew he was getting nearer to his home town of Rampur. The compulsion to return grew stronger. His motives for wishing to revisit Rampur so soon after his departure can only be a matter for conjecture. Perhaps it was a desire to take the fight to the enemy camp, perhaps no more than wistful curiosity.

At a village only two miles from Rampur, Sundar spent the day talking to the people. As it grew dark the villagers went to their homes. He found himself alone. Weary he lay down under a tree and tried to forget that he had eaten nothing that day. Should he seek out one of his listeners and ask for food? No, he had vowed never to beg. His thoughts turned to his home, less than an hour's walk away. At home he had never known hunger, never been cold. He checked his thoughts for he could see only too clearly their direction.

Suddenly his whole being was suffused by a sensation of peace and joy, and the tempting thoughts retreated. This was to happen to Sundar many times in his life. The more he endured and the greater his suffering, the more positively did he feel Christ's presence. So happy was he as he sat hungry and tired under the tree that he burst out singing and continued rejoicing until midnight. His voice echoed through the village. The people listened and crept out to see what he was doing. Perhaps he was drunk? Two of them approached the tree, and looked at him curiously. He was not drunk, but he seemed radiantly happy.

Sundar realised that his joyful outburst had been louder than he intended. He told his visitors why it was he sang.

"Forgive us," they said when he explained about his hunger. "We never thought. We will get you food at once." Sundar ate the food gratefully, thanked God for his care and lay down under his blanket. In no time he was asleep.

The next day as the light came he made his way to Rampur. He went, not to seek admission to his father's home with its food and shelter, but to tell the people of Rampur of the power and sustaining love of Jesus Christ.

A few months before he had been despised by the whole village, yet he found to his surprise a good audience amongst the shopkeepers and farm workers of Rampur. At last he seemed to be accepted by them. That evening, encouraged by his success, he made his way to his father's house. Even if he did not seek the comforts of his former home, he did hope for his father's blessing and understanding. At first his father refused to see him. Sundar sent a second request to his father, and was overjoyed when he caught sight of his father walking towards him.

"Very well, Sundar, you can stay here tonight; but you must leave early in the morning. After that I do not wish to see you again."

Sundar quietly joined his family, but he knew he was only barely tolerated. At the meal his father indicated that he should sit apart from the rest of them. He was afraid that his son might pollute the food or drinking vessels by his presence. It was painful for Sundar to be denied a place at his father's table and he felt the tears rising. He struggled to suppress them. Reluctantly they served him with some food. His father then approached him bearing a pitcher of water. To Sundar's great distress he saw his father lift the vessel high and pour the water into his son's hands from a great distance. Sundar could keep back his tears no longer. That was how high caste Indians gave water to an 'untouchable' or outcaste—the lowest rank of Hindu society.

Sundar rose to leave. "Father," he said, "it does not matter if you have forsaken me, because I have taken Christ for the love of Him who gave His life for me, and His love is unchangeable, and is far greater than yours. Before I became a Christian I dishonoured Christ, but he did not forsake me; now I do not complain. I thank you for your past love to me, and also for these past few hours under your roof."

Sundar bade his father good-bye and after a night in the open he left Rampur the next morning.

There are numerous stories that Sundar was later to relate concerning this period in his life. He kept no diary and it is impossible to know the exact order in which events occurred. His recollections do however give a vivid picture of the next four years when he went from village to village in north India preaching and teaching.

These few years can be regarded as an apprenticeship for his later work. His was essentially a ministry to individuals. He worked along person-to-person lines. Even the most casual encounter he regarded as an opportunity to evangelise.

We may question when we read of countless seemingly isolated incidents why he did not choose to spend more time in one place building up a firm Christian community. We wonder perhaps what became of his converts after his departure from the scene.

There are two things to bear in mind. We should not conclude on account of his individualistic approach that Sundar discounted the value of establishing local Christian groups. He invariably sent those who wished to make a firm Christian commitment to the nearest mission to be baptised and to receive further instruction, and thus to be supported during their ongoing Christian life. In military terms he saw himself as the advance guard.

Secondly, it was the more dramatic events of his life, the sudden conversions, the hair-raising escapes and the appalling privations that his contemporaries chose to record. The more pedestrian aspects of his life and ministry, the day-to-day love and support which he extended without stint, these not surprisingly failed to make the headlines. Doubtless whenever Sundar revisited a village he would seek out his earlier converts and assure himself of their well-being. He himself would value the opportunity whenever it occurred of encouraging and sharing in the corporate life of a local Christian community. It is with these thoughts in mind that we should study the tales of his adventures in north India during the period from 1905 to 1909.

He tells how he arrived at a village called Doliwala one evening on the point of exhaustion. He had been travelling all day and was anxious to find food and shelter. As the darkness fell, so did the rain. Sundar walked down the main street, the people clustered around him with offers of hospitality supposing him to be a Hindu sadhu. Sundar spoke of Jesus and then their greetings swiftly turned to threats. Wearily he stumbled towards the outskirts of the village with their abuse still ringing in his ears.

The rain became heavier and he was thankful to come across a derelict hut which afforded at least some shelter. Soaked and shivering though he was, he thanked God that he had found a place to rest and was asleep within minutes. He awoke cold and stiff in the half light of dawn. The sight of a black shadow lying close beside him on his blanket checked him as he was about to stretch his legs. He peered closer at the dark patch and recoiled in alarm. It was a huge black cobra that had settled down to sleep enjoying the warmth of Sundar's body. Trying not to make a sudden or jerky movement, he edged himself gently away from the terrifying black coil and then dashed out of the hut. The snake did not stir but lay heavily on Sundar's blanket. Thinking of the chill nights ahead, Sundar knew that the blanket could mean the difference between life and death. He crept back to the hut and eased the blanket from under its sinister weight. The black coil drowsily rearranged itself, but did nothing to prevent Sundar escaping with his blanket. God had saved him once again.

Travelling one day in the area around Meerut, Sundar told

a friend, Mr Alfred Zahir, how he had met a poor shepherd, cradling an injured lamb in his arms. The shepherd was sitting on a pile of stones by the road and Sundar came and sat beside him. The two fell into conversation. Despite his rough appearance the shepherd spoke to Sundar in a strangely confident and compelling manner. He stressed how his lambs taught him humility and how their obedience to their master was a lesson for all mankind. He spoke with rare insight for a peasant farmworker. Eventually the shepherd rose and wandered off leaving Sundar still sitting on the stones. Five minutes later Sundar followed hoping to catch him up. He spotted the shepherd ahead, disappearing behind a clump of trees and he hurried on to the place, but could see no sign of him. It was as if the shepherd had vanished into thin air.

"I am at a loss to tell where he disappeared," Sundar recounted to his friend. "I have not the least doubt that this man was an angel of God, who had been sent for my instruction, for the words he spoke went home to my heart, and I learnt such a lesson on humility and meekness as I shall never forget in all my life." An angel sent by God or a wise shepherd of flesh and blood? No one can answer that question but in one sense perhaps he was both.

At Jalalabad, Sundar met with a hostile response, but he was getting used to that and he did not feel unduly worried. The people were mostly Moslems and he hardly expected a welcome. While he was resting after talking to a group of them, a man cautiously approached him.

"You must go. There is a plot to kill you. They think you are a spy." His informant slipped away without another word. Sundar thought he had better take the advice. He gathered up his blanket and walked out of the village to the bare scrub beyond. It was no place to sleep in for it was infested with insects and exposed to cold winds, but Sundar had little choice.

He rested as best he could and in the morning he lit a fire to warm himself and to dry his clothes. He saw a group of men approaching him, and as they got nearer he recognised them as the Moslems he had met the day before, and about whom he had been warned. He stood up and faced them. Were they so determined to kill him that they sought him here? The men stopped a little way from him and murmured amongst themselves. One of them came closer and knelt down in front of him. Sundar was astonished. The man begged Sundar's forgiveness. They had wanted to kill him, he told Sundar, if he wasn't already dead from exposure after the cold night. Now that they had seen him alive and well they realised that he must be especially favoured of God. If Sundar would come back to Jalalabad with them, they would give him food and shelter and listen to his preaching. Sundar stayed with them a week, and felt that here at least he had made some headway.

A snake at Doliwala, a shepherd at Meerut, the Moslems at Jalalabad, three incidents out of many, but typical of Sundar Singh's experiences at that time. Danger from animals in that wild country was a constant part of his life, but always he came through safely. Often he was lonely and despondent but always the Lord upheld him. Hostility was the common reaction to his words, but time and again he was instrumental in bringing Christ alive for people as he did for the villagers at Jalalabad.

Why was it that a young man barely twenty years old, with no formal theological education or expertise could make such an impact even in the most unpromising conditions?

The answer lies partly in Sundar's personality and partly in his method of teaching. C. F. Andrews who first met him during these early years, later wrote of the impression Sundar Singh had made on him. He speaks of the 'wistful shyness' that Sundar had to master at their first meeting. It is fascinating to read his description of Sundar's appearance at that time, for such descriptions are few and far between.

> His face had the look of childhood fresh upon it, in spite of the marks of pain which were there also. At first sight, however, it was not so much his face that attracted my attention as his marvellous eyes. They were luminous, like the darkly gleaming water of some pool in the forest which a ray of sunlight has touched. While there was a shade of sorrow in them, there was also the light of joy and peace . . . In later years, the dignity of his presence deeply impressed me; but on that first occasion I seemed to see nothing but those eyes of his looking into my own and offering me his friendship. They seemed to tell me, without any formal words, how great a treasure his soul had found in Christ . . .

This was part of the secret. His love of God and his knowledge of God's saving love for him, seemed to shine out from his face. Again and again throughout his life people were to insist that being with him made them feel that they were in the very company of Christ. They were.

Like Jesus Christ he used parables in his teaching. The setting of his parables, again like Christ's, were drawn from the everyday life of his listeners and the sights and sounds of nature. This was an apt approach for his Indian audience for it was one with which they were familiar for Hindu teaching also employed a system of analogy.

For instance in elaborating the words of Jesus, "Ye are the salt of the earth", Sundar emphasised that a dry lump of salt cannot make rice palatable. It has to be dissolved. When dissolved it disappears and loses its identity. It is only in the taste of the rice that we know it has done its work. Thus must

Christians give of themselves. Lost to sight perhaps, but they will not be lost for they will live in the lives of others.

One major difference between Christianity and some branches of Hindu thought is the question of personal identity. To some Hindus the ultimate aim of man was to lose his personal identity and be absorbed by God and become part of God, a concept totally at variance with Christian belief. Sundar Singh likened a Christian's union with God to the way a bar of iron will become glowing red when placed in a furnace. It glows red because the fire penetrates it. Iron is not fire. Fire is not iron. So Jesus can live in us and transform us but we do not cease to be ourselves.

Travelling amongst the Himalayan mountains, Sundar Singh became deeply attached to the region, its beauty and its challenge. Many of his parables were gleaned from his close and accurate knowledge of the area.

"The streams in the Himalayan mountains," he said, "as they rush forth from the pure white snows, cut their own course. Each one has its own appointed path which it follows down the mountainside. That rushing torrent of pure water from the heights is the true symbol of the Christian life as it comes direct from Christ Himself.

"But when the same waters reach the plains, they carry the mud along with them, and their tributaries are diverted into channels by artificial means, forming irrigation canals. These too have their uses, but they depend on the streams which flow from the mountain heights for their perennial supply of fresh living water." In other words he was saying that man-made 'irrigation' (i.e. aspects of the institutional church) had value. Yet, nonetheless, those channels were entirely dependent on 'flooding' by the grace of the Spirit if they were to function effectively.

It was Sundar's practice to work and travel alone, but for a year he had a companion. In August 1906 he met an American layman, Samuel Stokes. Stokes had come to India to preach Christianity but had not felt drawn to work with any of the recognised missionary societies. On meeting Sundar, he felt at once that the sadhu's way of living was appropriate for India. He and Sundar decided to join forces and to travel and work together.

Their first night was spent at Jammu, a town lying in the foothills of the Himalayas about one hundred miles north of Lahore. They were offered neither food nor proper shelter, although eventually they were given permission to sleep in a filthy cowshed and were handed a loaf of stale bread. The cowshed was chilly and infested with bugs. They got no sleep that night, but remembering Our Lord's birth in the Bethlehem stable they spent the time praying together.

The dominant factor in bringing Samuel Stokes to India and to the life of a homeless wanderer had been the example of Saint Francis of Assisi. Thus at a time when Sundar was still developing his ideal of the sadhu-life, Stokes introduced another important element, the idea of service to man going hand in hand with the service of God.

Throughout his life, Sundar sought to unite his desire for solitude, the need to be alone with God, with his belief that in serving man we also serve God.

During this first preaching tour together Sundar's health broke down. He had severe abdominal pains and ran a high temperature. Stokes became anxious for his friend. They were many miles from the nearest village and Stokes was sure that Sundar would not be able to travel much farther. Sundar finally collapsed by the roadside, almost unconscious with pain. Stokes eased him into a more comfortable position. Sundar's eyes opened. "How are you?" inquired Stokes. A low voice answered, "I am very happy; how sweet it is to suffer for His sake."

Stokes was in a dilemma. No one would pass by on that lonely path. He had to leave Sundar and find help. Fortunately a European planter's house was only a few miles away. Stokes got help and Sundar was carried there. The owner insisted they should both stay until Sundar was better. He was much impressed by these two young men, and their quiet confident faith. As Sundar recovered they had many discussions and in time the planter was converted.

Sundar and Samuel made their way to the Leper Hospital at Sabathu, the place Sundar had stayed before his baptism. No doubt seeking to put their ideal into practice, they spent a month working amongst the lepers. Even during their rest periods they remained with the patients. Despite the risk to their own health they did not spare themselves in comforting the sick and dying.

Shortly after this, Stokes returned to America planning to recruit more men to join their work. Sundar Singh and Stokes were never again to work so closely together even when Stokes came back to India. Yet they both tried each summer to snatch a few weeks together when it was their custom to take crippled children from the hospital up to a summer camp in the mountains.

4

TIBET HAD NOT been forgotten by Sundar Singh. The Himalayan peaks, silent and still in the distance beyond Sabathu, constantly beckoned him. Tibetan traders with their inscrutable Eastern features, their prayer wheels and their long-haired yaks, mingled with the native population in the border towns and villages north-east of Simla. They were a constant reminder of that enclosed and forbidding land.

The Hindustan-Tibet road climbed high above the River Sutlej. As Sundar began his first journey to Tibet along that road he could see the river far below winding like a silver thread through the trees. The road swept down into the sultry valley, past the town of Rampur. This was not the Rampur where Sundar was born, but a trading post where even the architecture spoke of Tibet. Out of Rampur, the road degenerated into a track. Clinging to the steep mountainsides it made its way up and up, higher and higher. The temperature dropped sharply. It was lonely. Sundar Singh had reached Lesser Tibet.

The Moravian Church had already penetrated this far, and when Sundar reached their mission station at Poo, he was welcomed by the two missionaries there, Kunick and Marx, who pressed Sundar to stay briefly with them. They were able to teach him the rudiments of the Tibetan language. Sundar's plans caught their imagination and anxious to encourage him, they promised that a young Christian layman from the mission, Tarnyed Ali, should accompany him. Sundar accepted gladly. He was already beginning to sense the alien nature of the country, and a companion and guide who knew the language would be a comfort and an asset.

The two young men set off up the mountain track, deeper and deeper into Tibet. All that he saw filled Sundar with despair and shock. The people were dirty, superstitious and ignorant. Their food was poor, their homes as evil-smelling as their owners. At Kiwar village, Sundar and Tarnyed Ali were driven out because its inhabitants were so disgusted to see them washing themselves and their clothes in a stream. A local lama who witnessed this spectacle told the people, "It is all right for sinful men to wash their clothes, but for good people to do so is very bad."

Later Sundar was to record how in one place, Lara, he saw a man who was quite black from dirt, and who obviously could not have had a bath for a decade. "The people's clothes," he wrote, "although made of white wool, from filth look as if they were made of black leather because they never wash them."

Food was an even worse problem. The mainstay of their diet was dried barley, which was so hard and indigestible that even animals had been known to refuse it. For drink there was Tibetan tea which is mixed with salt and rancid butter.

Everywhere the prayer wheels turned bearing the mystic words, '*Om mane padme hum*', impossible to translate literally since each syllable denotes a whole range of meaning, and the meaning of the whole is greater than the meaning of its component parts. It was hardly fertile ground for a Christian preacher. The points of contact were so few.

On this first visit, although their reception in the villages was decidedly cool, they were never physically ill-treated. Sundar and Tarnyed, however, were left in no doubt that the preaching of Christianity would not be tolerated in this Buddhist stronghold. The lamas were strongly entrenched and their authority absolute. Since the peasants lived in fear of them, there was little chance for any stranger to gain a hearing.

The important centre of Tashigang boasted a Chief Lama, a man with jurisdiction over numerous subordinate priests. Here, expecting the usual enmity, Sundar and his companion were surprised by a warm welcome. Evidently the Chief Lama of Tashigang must have been a man of liberal sympathies. They were given food and shelter and invited to speak to the people. Only very occasionally did they meet such friendliness.

Once they were threatened with the words, "If you do not stop troubling us, the same treatment will be given to you as was meted out to Kartar Singh."

Sundar was to hear the name Kartar Singh again and again, but it was not until they met a Tibetan convert to Christianity that they learned the whole story of Kartar's witness and martyrdom. It transpired that Kartar Singh's early history was remarkably similar to Sundar's. Both came from the same Sikh country. Both had been turned out of their homes by their fathers. Both had refused to renounce their Christian faith. Kartar Singh on finding himself without home, clothes or money had worked as a labourer until he could buy for himself the yellow robe of a sadhu. Tibet called to him as it was later to call to Sundar Singh, and for three months he preached there about Jesus. The people, egged on by the lamas, grew more and more aggressive. He was brought before the Head Lama of the area and charged with teaching a foreign religion.

Since their Buddhist religion forbids the taking of life, the Tibetans had devised their own sadistic punishments, which inevitably ended in the death of the victim but relieved the instigators of direct responsibility. So it was that Kartar Singh was sentenced to be sewn into a wet yak skin which was to be left in the sun to dry and shrink, thus squeezing the prisoner to death. This Kartar Singh endured, praying and singing all the while. On the fourth day, knowing death was near, he asked to have his right hand freed so that he could write in the flyleaf of his New Testament which lay beside him. He wrote a verse praising God. With his last ounce of strength he spoke to the people.

"Are you standing by to see the death of a Christian? Come and gaze attentively, that not a Christian but death itself dies here. Oh Lord! into thy hands I commend my spirit because it is thine."

Those were to be his last words on earth. One of those who had observed his martyrdom was the lama's personal secretary. He picked up the dead man's New Testament and took it home. He turned its pages curiously. What was Kartar Singh's inspiration that he died so bravely? As the secretary read he became more and more impressed and soon began to tell others of what he had found.

The lama was angry. Kartar Singh's punishment was to have deterred people from taking Christianity seriously and here was one of his own men actually converted to these pernicious beliefs by witnessing this Christian's death. The secretary could expect no mercy and did not receive it. He was cruelly beaten and his wounded body was left for dead on a rubbish dump outside the town. But he did not die. Strength came to crawl away and slowly his wounds healed. Courageously he went back to the town and the people cowered away from him for they were deeply fearful of the power that had given life to one they thought was dead. From that time onwards he was left alone and allowed to preach unmolested. It was he who told Sundar of Kartar Singh's death.

The story of these two brave men moved Sundar greatly. Often he was to tell their tale. On Patiala railway station while speaking to a group after his return from Tibet, he noticed a man with tears running down his face standing on the fringe of the crowd. It was Kartar Singh's father, who had turned his son out of his home, and who had had no news of him since that day. Sundar Singh's story of his son's brave death, and indeed Sundar himself, so like his son in many ways, had a profound effect on the old man, who himself was to become a Christian.

Their first tour of Tibet was nearly ended. Sundar and Tarnyed Ali made their way home. Soon the snow would block the mountain passes and travel would be impossible.

Sundar now knew for certain that God was calling him to further work in Tibet. Until his disappearance twenty years later in that same treacherous land, he was to make many such journeys. The melting of the snows in the spring and early summer were a yearly signal to make ready for another visit.

It was two years since Sundar's baptism, two years that had matured him. He had proved himself in his God-given vocation. His body had become hardened against the discomforts he daily faced. In discomfort, in danger, in speaking of his faith, in exhaustion, in suffering hostility, he had felt God's presence and known his guidance.

Shy and reserved though he was, he had a serene confidence, the mark of an inner strength. It impressed others, among them, Susil Rudra and Charles F. Andrews, whose acquaintance Sundar made shortly after his first visit to Tibet.

Susil Rudra, an Indian, was the Principal of St Stephen's College, Delhi. This was a Christian institution providing university education for boys from the Punjab. The Reverend Charles Andrews, an English missionary, was on the staff of the college and a great friend of Rudra's with whom he lodged. At the beginning of the long vacation in 1907 the two men, with Susil's sons, Sudhir and Ajit, were making for Kotgarh, about twenty-five miles beyond Simla. The long vacation stretched before them, and they thankfully left behind the heat of the plains.

Kotgarh lies just off the Hindustan–Tibet road where it

passes through a massive pine forest. In a clearing, there was a church, a school, a hospital, a handful of houses, orchards and fields of corn, and that was Kotgarh. It was a welcome contrast to the bustling activity of Delhi.

Here in Kotgarh Susil Rudra and Charles Andrews first met Sundar Singh. Their common faith was an immediate bond. Although the solitary figure in his saffron robe was shy at first, a firm and lasting friendship took root. Sundar Singh's life and ministry as a sadhu found an enthusiastic response in the two men from Delhi. Susil was a second generation Christian. His father, Piyare Mohan Rudra had, after becoming a Christian, determined to remain loyal to the Hindu tradition except where that tradition was clearly in conflict with Christian precepts. He was therefore regarded with suspicion by Hindu and Christian alike. Susil had followed the same lonely path and knew its humiliations. When he met Sundar he could from his own experience readily understand the sacrifices this young man had made. To them both, the future direction of the Indian Church was a matter of passionate concern. Sundar was overjoyed to find as a friend another Indian who saw as distinctly as he did the need for the Christian Church in India to evolve its own identity.

Charles F. Andrews despite his own European background shared Susil's views and he too was deeply influenced by Sundar Singh's outlook. In later years when there was, amongst expatriate clergy, much opposition to the growing national movement in India, Andrews spoke and wrote strongly in support of Gandhi and outspokenly criticised the British administration and what he called 'the Western captivity' of the Indian Church.

A highlight of their annual summer vacations at Kotgarh was their meeting with Sundar. Often they found him with the groups of children that he brought up from Sabathu for a holiday, and they noticed his spontaneous rapport with children. Susil's own children, Sudhir and Ajit, were devoted to him, and would eagerly greet him and ply him with questions the moment they met.

Charles Andrews recalled one occasion when they were at Kotgarh. "Sundar got up one night from prayer and was preparing to go out alone. When questioned why he was starting so late at night, he replied that he had heard the call of someone from the valley below who was needing his immediate help. Those who were sleeping by his side implored him to wait until the early dawn and not risk the dangers of the forest throughout the night. But the Sadhu insisted on starting at that very moment. After a few days he returned. The person he had gone to seek had been seriously ill and had greatly needed his assistance."

Susil Rudra and Charles Andrews urged Sundar to visit them at the college in Delhi, and this he often did. They had another reason for encouraging his visits apart from the pleasure and inspiration of his company. They were at this time concerned about the quality of college life.

If a boy from a Christian home could pass his matriculation exam, and the standard required was not particularly high, he could easily qualify for a place. The college was well endowed and it was this easy availability of resources which paradoxically presented a problem. With so much provided, the students tended to see themselves as a privileged *élite*. From among these boys would come the future leaders in Church and State. Their school career should have prepared them for the demands and disciplines of public life. Instead they came to expect status and reward as their due. That this should be the case in a Christian college was a cause of great regret to Principal Rudra and Charles Andrews. The latter admitted with candour that his own life-style as a teacher was hardly likely to impress students as an example of austerity and self-denial.

Yet Sundar Singh on his visits, though himself little older than the students, set before them an ideal of Christianity in its Indian context. Whenever he stayed with Susil he spent hours talking with the students and his influence upon them for good was immense. One gave up his prospect of lucrative government service to work as a Christian teacher; another nursed one of the college servants, a man of the lowest caste, through an illness, unprecedented behaviour; a third carried a peasant, suffering from an infectious disease, several miles over a rough mountain track to get him to a doctor.

The friendship of the three men continued throughout their lives. When Andrews left Delhi for Bengal he rarely met Sundar although their friendship continued firm, but Susil, until his death in 1924, remained in touch with him.

Shoran Singh was another young man who came under Sundar's influence at this time, and was later to become a Y.M.C.A. Secretary in London. He recalls an incident from those times when they were staying together. Late one evening they noticed lights moving in the valley. Sundar thought that a leopard hunt was in progress. In the early hours of the morning Shoran Singh was disturbed by a noise in the room, and saw Sundar get up and go out. Shoran was not surprised for he knew that the sadhu often kept a prayer vigil during the night. On this occasion however Shoran felt apprehensive. From a window he saw Sundar standing near some trees in the moonlight. Even as he watched he saw a long, low, slinking shadow move silently towards Sundar. It was a leopard. Panic seized Shoran. He could neither move nor speak. He watched transfixed as Sundar turned absentmindedly towards the animal and patted its head as though it was a dog.

Sundar seemed to have a strange power over animals. There

is no record of his ever having been harmed by one despite many perilous encounters.

In similar vein is his experience at Thoria. Here he was forced to spend the night in a jungle cave, so hostile were the people. He awoke to find a leopard lying at his side. Without disturbing the sleeping animal, Sundar crept out of the cave unharmed.

On leaving another unwelcoming village, Sundar climbed on to a rock to rest. He saw that he was being watched by a black panther. "What shall I do?" thought Sundar. "If I move the panther may pounce. Yet I can't stay here for ever." He prayed for God's guidance and protection, and then got down from the rock and walked with such confidence as he could muster back to the village and away from the panther. The villagers were curious.

"Why have you come back here again? We thought we'd seen the last of you."

Sundar described his miraculous escape and as his story unfolded so their attentiveness increased. One who had been spared from that same panther which had already killed several local men must be possessed of extraordinary holiness.

Stories such as these spread from village to village. Tibet was accessible for only a few months in the year so a large proportion of Sundar's year was spent wandering in north-east India, where he went from one village to another seeking an audience.

At Narkanda, midway between Simla and Kotgarh, Sundar stopped to talk to reapers working in the fields. Anxious to complete their harvest while the good weather held, they had no time to listen to preachers. Indignation rose when they discovered Sundar was a Christian. One of them hurled a stone at him and cut his head. The others looked up expecting a torrent of curses and abuse, but they heard instead his gentle voice murmuring, "Father, forgive them." He washed his injured head in a stream. The man who had cast the stone began to complain of a headache and eventually had to give up reaping and go home.

Quietly Sundar took up the man's scythe and joined them in their work. All that day in the hot sun he laboured with them. Gratitude overcame their resistance and they asked him to come home with them and rest. That night at the house of a man called Nandi, brother to the one who had attacked him, Sundar talked to an eager audience about his Christian faith.

The next day he bade them good-bye, but his message was not forgotten and they wished they could hear more. They were further disconcerted on discovering that the part of the field which Sundar had reaped had produced a greater yield than ever before. Nandi was still full of the story when he met a friend some weeks later. He told Jiya Ram what had occurred, and how they wished to meet Sundar Singh again. Jiya was impressed; he had already heard tales of Sundar Singh and his compelling sanctity and he decided to write to the *Nur Afshan*, a north Indian newspaper, and through its columns appeal to Sundar to return to Narkanda.

There is no record whether Sundar ever saw the newspaper but it is most likely he did return to Narkanda as it lay close by a road he often travelled.

On another road of the region Sundar noticed two men hurrying ahead of him. He lost sight of them as they rounded a bend, and when the road straightened again, only one was to be seen. He pointed with wild gesticulations towards a figure lying beneath a sheet on the ground. Sundar was somewhat surprised at the suddenness of this demise but agreed to give the distraught survivor all the money he had on him for the burial expenses. There was nothing else he could do to help so Sundar continued along the road. The sound of pounding footsteps behind him made him turn around. There stood the dead man's friend weeping even more profusely.

"He really is dead," he sobbed.

"Yes, you told me before that he was dead," said Sundar gently, feeling somewhat puzzled.

"It was a trick. We often did it. One of us would pretend to be dead and the other would persuade passers-by to part with burial money. We would take it in turns to play the part of the dead man. When you left I lifted the sheet and I found he really had died. I should never have deceived a holy man like you." He wiped his tears and added, "Thank goodness it was not my turn to be the dead man!"

Sundar comforted him and explained he was a Christian sadhu. When he told him that God could forgive him and his friend, the man was keen to hear more. At the end of their discussion, he asked Sundar if he would baptise him. This was something Sundar would not do. He explained that it would be better if the man went to the mission station at Garhwal which was not far away. There he would receive further teaching and could become part of the local worshipping community.

The fame of Sundar spread throughout the region as the stories multiplied. Sundar however had no desire for his own name to become famous. It was the name of Jesus Christ alone which mattered. God had given to Sundar a rare and precious gift. The ability to communicate powerfully to others the faith which had transformed his life.

Friends while acknowledging this innate ability considered none the less that his ministry would profit from some formal evangelistic training. The Bishop of Lahore, Dr Lefroy, had watched Sundar's career with growing appreciation. The Bishop wanted to put before Sundar the possibility of ordination for he felt that within the ordained ministry his contribution to the Indian Church would be invaluable.

It was with this in mind that in 1909, when Sundar was in his twentieth year, the Bishop suggested that he should attend Saint John's Divinity School, Lahore.

5

HIS FELLOW STUDENTS at the Divinity College regarded him with a mixture of awe and suspicion. Sundar regarded them in much the same way. In their eyes he was an oddity. He continued to wear his sadhu's robe since it had not occurred to him that theological training would in any way interfere with his vocation to live the life of a Christian sadhu. He was by nature quiet and reserved, but to the students his manner appeared stand-offish. His spiritual disciplines, although unostentatious, reflected unfavourably on the Christian commitment of many of the students, for whom long hours of prayer and meditation were not deemed a necessary accompaniment to their vocation. What was equally questionable in the eyes of the students was that Sundar came with a reputation. He was already an established figure in Christian circles. Whereas most students presented themselves to the Bishop seeking ordination, it was the Bishop who had suggested the idea to Sundar.

Thus Sundar found himself in an atmosphere of misgiving and distrust. He was used to hostility in Tibet, he was used to hostility in Indian villages, but here, in a Christian college, surely he would be accepted. He remembered the Christian Boys' College at Ludhiana, where the casual attitudes of the pupils had shocked him. They too had seemed to take their discipleship lightly.

Once more he pondered the Brahmin priest's brass bowl and the parable it had suggested to him. All his convictions that the Water of Life, the redemptive love of Jesus Christ, must be presented to the people of India in an Indian vessel, were reinforced. Was the training that the Church offered the young men at the college appropriate for a ministry in India?

The question, together with his uneasy position vis-à-vis the other students, made this period of Sundar Singh's life a frustrated and unhappy one.

Bishop Lefroy, in suggesting theological training for Sundar, had perhaps had similar doubts about the European orientation of the Indian Church, and hoped that Sundar might embody for the Church a pattern of Indian priesthood. Sundar respected the Bishop's confidence in him and resisted the temptation to leave the college.

For the most part he found the lectures irrelevant to Christ's teaching. A distrust of abstract theological argument was to remain with him for the rest of his life.

Charles Andrews visited Sundar Singh at the college whenever he could get to Lahore and has recorded this impression: "He seemed to me like some bird of the forest, beating its wings in vain against the bars of a cage. For the joyous, open freedom at Kotgarh, with the clear sky overhead and solitude of the hills round about, had been left behind. It was almost as if his wings had been clipped, and I felt deeply distressed about him when I saw what was happening, as though a tragedy was being acted out before my eyes."

It was to Charles Andrews that Sundar recounted an incident which marked an improvement in his relations with the other students. He had been puzzled and saddened by their antagonistic attitude. Accordingly Sundar had prayed that he might make amends for his part in the discord which existed. In particular he prayed for one boy who had been his most vociferous critic. This same boy heard Sundar at his prayers and was amazed to hear his own name on Sundar's lips. He felt a genuine sense of shame and there and then approached Sundar.

"Forgive me," he said, "my attitude to you has been thoroughly uncharitable." Almost from this moment a close friendship between the two took root. Gradually Sundar felt himself more at home in the college.

Charles Andrews met the student in question years later who verified the story and declared how this occurrence and his subsequent friendship with Sundar Singh had coloured his whole ministry.

Thus his three terms at Saint John's were not entirely wasted. Even his studies introduced him to writers like Thomas à Kempis whose *Imitation of Christ* he read and re-read throughout his life.

At the end of the year Sundar left the college with a licence to preach and it was assumed that he would eventually go on to receive deacon's orders. Samuel Stokes had returned from America and was in the process of founding a Franciscan Brotherhood. Sundar was interested and encouraging. Although he did not join the community, he attended the service in Lahore Cathedral at which Stokes and another member made their vows. Sundar was not able to commit himself to any such organisation. He had other plans.

The hot weather had begun as the Divinity College term ended, and Sundar was anxious to get to Tibet, to the work he felt called to do. This proposal caused consternation in some quarters. Had he not just received a licence to preach in the Anglican churches in the Diocese of Lahore? For that reason he could not just set off in whatever direction he chose. Furthermore as a priest or deacon he would be committed to working within the Anglican Communion and within one diocese of that Communion.

It is strange that a whole year at the college had passed without this issue being raised. Neither Bishop Lefroy, nor the staff at Saint John's, nor Sundar himself had hitherto faced this question. Sundar seemed to have believed that neither a preacher's licence nor ordination would in any way limit his work as an itinerant evangelist. He now had to face the fact that other people had quite different ambitions for him.

At this particular crossroad he knew what he must do. His only regret as he returned his preacher's licence to the Bishop, was a reluctance to disappoint Dr Lefroy who had been a good friend to him. The Bishop, however, accepted Sundar's reasons, acknowledging generously that he had been mistaken in his plans for the young man.

For Sundar the renunciation of his licence had not been difficult, yet it does symbolise that his was a ministry that knew no sectarian bounds. His calling was to preach to the non-Christian. He gladly left to others within the Church the important work of building up the established Christian community.

Like John Wesley he regarded the world as his parish. He remained an Anglican by virtue of his baptism and confirmation. He had been confirmed by Bishop Lefroy in 1907 at Kotgarh. Throughout his life he remained a communicant and was a regular preacher in Anglican churches. But he would not be bound by a denominational allegiance and when he felt it appropriate to step outside its conventions he showed no compunction in doing so.

The world of Matins and Evensong, Chapter Meetings and Diocesan Committees was wholly foreign to Sundar. His world was the rugged terrain of Tibet and the giving of his whole being to the preaching of his Master's word. It was a world where life itself was constantly at risk; equally it was a world where God would send his angels to rescue his servants from danger.

Sundar did not find his many miraculous escapes matters to be wondered at. They simply indicated that God still had work for him to do, so he gave thanks for his safety and forged ahead once more. This carefree approach was leagues away from cautious institutional Christianity although it was not so far removed from traditional Indian spirituality.

The modern student of Sundar Singh's life must interpret his many escapes from death and danger according to his own convictions. In particular incidents the succour, which Sundar regarded as the direct intervention of God on his behalf, will seem to others to be the workings of nature or coincidence. Taken as a whole, however, few would deny that his life seemed to be remarkably protected. Were the mysterious figures who appeared in times of difficulty or danger men or angels? It was God's care that they exemplified. The ways and means are of minor significance.

One such escape occurred in Nepal, the mountainous region that lies between Tibet and India. The angry inhabitants of the village of Khantzi had seized and assaulted Sundar. Wrapped in a blanket he was bound tightly to a fruit tree outside the village. His persecutors waited for him to die. They were sure he would. If the leeches and the scorpions and the snakes failed, a leopard would no doubt succeed. Sundar fainted with pain. On recovering consciousness he awoke to find he was no longer tied to the tree. His wounds had been tended and in his hands were fruits from the tree. Sundar thanked God that he had been delivered from death and was encouraged to continue on his journey.

In his wanderings through India and Tibet, Sundar continually faced the prospect of sudden death. For his Master he was happy to do so. He was equally happy to be spared for further work. This sort of life was, he believed, God's intention for him, not parochial work in an Anglican mission station.

So, on leaving Saint John's College in 1910, he returned to the life of a wandering preacher, taking whatever opportunities God put in his way to preach to those who had not heard the Christian Gospel.

It was during these years that the Reverend Thomas Ewart Riddle first met him. A New Zealand Presbyterian minister, he came as a missionary to the Punjab early in 1912 and was to remain, apart from a period of war service, until 1947. Thomas Riddle was to become Sundar's lifelong friend. He was his executor and it was he who organised the search party that tried to trace Sundar when he disappeared in 1929.

In 1946 Thomas Riddle wrote a series of articles on Sundar Singh in successive issues of *The United Church Review*, a paper of which he was the editor. These articles were later put together in a book called *The Vision and the Call* which was published in India. In the issue for June 1946 he recounts an incident which in Sundar's eyes was a case of direct intervention by God on his behalf, but which in the view of his companion, had quite a different explanation.

In a lonely jungle area, Sundar and his friend Samuel Stokes had reached a fast-flowing river. There seemed no way to cross except by swimming. Sundar waded into the water, started to swim and was striking out powerfully for the other side when the sheer force of the current swept him down the river towards treacherous rapids. Stokes watched with horror from the bank, powerless to help. Suddenly he looked across to the far side to see a party of hillmen running alongside the river. After slithering down the bank, between them, they pulled Sundar out. That was how Stokes recalled the episode. Yet when Sundar told of his escape he said, "I saw in that instant that God had sent his angels to snatch me from sure death."

Whether Stokes or whether Sundar was right we shall never know. Does one version exclude the other? Probably not. Others in moments of extreme danger have sensed the divine presence. There is the well-known story of Sir Ernest Shackleton's experience in his perilous journey across South Georgia in search of civilisation and help for his companions left marooned on a small, bleak island. He wrote, "I know that during that long and racking march of thirty-six hours over the unnamed mountains and glaciers of South Georgia it seemed to me often that we were four, not three. I said nothing to my companions on the point, but afterwards Worsley said to me, 'Boss, I had a curious feeling on the march that there was another person with us.' Crean confessed to the same idea."

Those who knew Sundar Singh never doubted his integrity, when he related his experiences. However, as Thomas Riddle points out in his articles, some of Sundar's listeners felt that such instances of divine intervention occurred during bouts of fatigue and weariness when the 'borders between fact and fancy are blurred'.

There were however others who, as Sundar's fame spread, were convinced that he was an impostor, and used these, as they saw them, extravagant tales of miraculous delivery as proof of their argument. Neither was Sundar helped by the over-enthusiastic support of his more fervent admirers. Anxious to extol their hero they freely circulated details of his life that he would have preferred to conceal from public curiosity.

The summer of 1912 found Sundar once more in Tibet. He chose a route through the border town of Tehri and made for Lake Manasarowar, a region of solitary and mysterious beauty. High above the lake, the haunt of wild swans, tower rocky precipices crowned with ancient Buddhist temples, remote and deserted. Towards this region, Sundar journeyed across the Kailash mountain range. For generations of Hindus, Kailash had held sacred associations. Although the area had the outward appearance of total desertion it was not entirely uninhabited. Sundar had heard rumours of holy Hindu hermits who had chosen for themselves lives of solitary meditation, and he had always hoped that one day he might meet one, though he regarded the prospect as unlikely, particularly in that desolate area. In fact he wrote in *A Collection of Incidents*, a book about his travels written in Urdu, "I had not the slightest conception that anyone could live in so bleak a place."

The path he was following was treacherous even for Sundar who was by now a hardened and experienced traveller in such conditions. His foot slipped on a patch of ice and he fell down heavily several feet to a lower level. Momentarily stunned he opened his eyes and noticed to his alarm a figure sitting close by at the entrance to a cave. Sundar recoiled in fear at the sight. It was an incredibly old man, with matted hair down to his shoulders. The figure addressed him in somewhat strange terms.

"Before we begin to converse together it will be well for us to pray to God." Sundar's fears receded a little and he watched intently while the old man fetched an ancient book from his cave, sat down and began to read aloud. Sundar strained to catch his words. To his amazement he heard the old man read from the New Testament, part of the Sermon on the Mount. Not only had he come across a hermit, but a Christian hermit at that. Sundar was anxious to know how he'd become a believer.

Here is Sundar's account of the old man's reply as he recorded it in *A Collection of Incidents*, written early in 1915:

> He said: "My birth was in Alexandria. When I was thirty years of age, Jarnos, the nephew of Saint Francis Xavier, baptised me . . . Up to my seventy-fifth year I preached in the whole world. I spoke twenty-one languages well. When I knew that I could no longer travel about, I gradually made my way to this place. I have been living here for two hundred and nine years. God has committed to

me the ministry of prayer, that I should pray for different places in turn."

He went on to tell Sundar that he believed that Christ's coming was imminent, that Christ would reign for one thousand years visibly on earth, after which there would be the resurrection and judgment of sinners.

Sundar was deeply moved with the hermit's words. If he entertained any doubts concerning the Maharishi's (Indian word meaning a 'great seer') claim that he could move in spirit throughout the world as he prayed, these doubts were removed when the Maharishi told him many things about his own life and friends, that he could not possibly have been expected to know.

Sundar continued his account:

> Afterwards more conversation followed . . . It is hoped that when some friends go with me to meet with him a complete and detailed account may be written, along with a picture of the venerable saint. Inhabited dwellings begin at a distance of about eighty miles from where the Maharishi lives. His food consists of various forest roots, which are exceedingly strength-giving . . . One more amazing thing he mentioned to me and prophetically said that within a short time a wonderful occurrence would happen to me which would greatly strengthen my faith.

To illustrate the Maharishi's strange foresight, Sundar goes on in his book to tell how, on his way down from Mount Kailash, he met a group of people who deliberately misdirected him when they realised he was a Christian. He had inquired the route to the nearest village, but they had sent him instead along a hazardous forest path.

Night soon enveloped the landscape. There was no sign of a village. Sundar could hear the cries of wild animals in the jungle around him. At length he reached a river, but it flowed too swiftly for him to wade across. The prospect looked bleak, and Sundar was near despair.

A light on the far bank attracted his attention. A man was sitting by a fire. He stood up and called across to Sundar.

"Do not be troubled. I am coming to get you." To Sundar's surprise the man did exactly that. After wading through the river he carried Sundar on his shoulders back to the far side. Safe across the river, Sundar turned to thank his guide. He was no longer there. Nor could he find any trace of the fire. Sundar remembered the Maharishi's prophecy.

A hermit three hundred years old, a prophecy so explicitly fulfilled. Do such things happen in the twentieth century? What are we to make of them?

Sundar was to meet the Maharishi on two further occasions. The stories of these encounters with the Maharishi of Kailash are perplexing to the modern reader. A host of questions are raised. For instance there are those relating to the claim by the Maharishi that he was baptised by a nephew of Saint Francis Xavier. On his own reckoning the Maharishi had been born two hundred and eighty-four years before he first met Sundar in 1912. The year of his birth therefore would have been 1628. Francis Xavier lived from 1506 until 1552 and was the youngest of five children. Had the Maharishi at the age of thirty been baptised by a nephew of Saint Francis Xavier this would have taken place in 1658, one hundred and six years after the saint's death. Moreover it is known that Saint Francis had almost nothing to do with his family after he left home in 1525. Do these considerations discredit the historical accuracy of the story? Could Sundar have dreamed the whole thing while unconscious from his fall? If so, how can his subsequent meetings with the Maharishi be explained?

The questions are endless and they have all been asked. Sundar's critics certainly questioned his integrity in the matter. How did his friends regard the affair?

Charles Andrews gives us a hint of the way Sundar's friend, Susil Rudra, felt about it.

> Now and then he [Susil Rudra] was perplexed by the strange narratives which the Sadhu brought back concerning his wanderings in Tibet, and he would often argue with him that much of what he had experienced had been due to his highly wrought imagination. He doubted some of the stories, but he never doubted for a moment the sincerity and simplicity of the Sadhu himself. That was beyond question.

The views of another personal friend, Aiyadurai Jesudasen Appasamy, who was to become Sundar Singh's chief biographer, are very relevant here. A. J. Appasamy, later Bishop in Coimbatore and a man with immense knowledge of Indian Christianity, went to considerable lengths in his book *Sundar Singh* (1958) to find a satisfactory answer to this controversy. He concluded that there were three legitimate ways of regarding Sundar's experiences with the Maharishi.

There is the possibility that he fabricated the whole story, but as Bishop Appasamy points out, lifelong friends could testify to his truthfulness. Furthermore Sundar was very willing to take others to see the Maharishi. Two such expeditions did in fact set out but neither of them achieved their destination.

Secondly, it could be argued that Sundar saw the Maharishi in a vision. As he grew older ecstatic experiences became a frequent occurrence in his spiritual life. However the visions he saw while in a state of ecstasy usually served to illuminate a specific problem that was troubling him at the time. Life after death was something which particularly exercised his mind and most of his visions illuminated his difficulties on this very subject.

Lastly there is the possibility that Sundar did see a very old hermit praying in a cave near Mount Kailash. Reports from travellers who had sighted such people were quite frequent. An American mining engineer reported that he had seen such an old man, and the Reverend Yunas Singh of the London Missionary Society was told in 1916 by Tibetan traders about a 'very, very old Rishi' who lived in the Kailish mountains just below the snowline.

It seems likely therefore, as Bishop Appasamy says, that Sundar did meet the Maharishi, who may indeed have been very old, old enough perhaps to be somewhat confused about his true age.

Sundar had no wish to arouse speculation concerning the Maharishi, and when Alfred Zahir's book with its highly-coloured narratives provoked curiosity Sundar was troubled. He became reluctant to discuss the Maharishi at all. Bishop Appasamy records that when he first met Sundar Singh in Oxford in 1920, the sadhu was pressed at a meeting to give more details of the Maharishi. He replied to his questioners, "People have made too much of this incident in my life. The Maharishi is a man of prayer and I have a great respect for him; but my work is not to preach the Rishi, but to preach Christ."

Sundar's attitude puts the matter into perspective, and again, we must not forget that this was India, where conceptions of reality are rooted in a culture quite different from that of the pragmatic West. Sundar was part of that culture. He understood it and appreciated it. He was completely Indian and could therefore speak to India.

Here perhaps lies the strongest justification for his decision not to be ordained as a deacon in the Church of England. Had he done so his work would have been mainly amongst those who had embraced not only Christianity but a European mode of life. Sundar's message was to all men, and certainly to his fellow Indians.

He was never afraid to preach even at Hindu shrines. On one occasion he began to talk to pilgrims by the Ganges who, when they realised he was a Christian, fetched a Hindu sadhu to refute his arguments. On arrival he approached Sundar and to the bewilderment of the bystanders, placed his two forefingers in Sundar's mouth.

"I have done this to prove that we are brothers and not enemies as you suppose, for we both believe in Jesus Christ as Saviour."

Sundar was greatly encouraged and spent some hours talking to the sadhu. He discovered that this man believed that it was better to evangelise secretly in the guise of a Hindu, since he was able to introduce his Christian conviction without arousing hostility. He had already baptised several people. It was not the way Sundar cared to proceed but he respected his friend's point of view.

6

"TEACHER, TEACHER, HERE comes Jesus, here comes Jesus!" With these words a little girl burst into the study of the Principal of the Pool Girls' High School in Osaka, Japan. She was referring to Sundar Singh who was walking outside in the school grounds.

This incident did not take place until 1919 when Sundar, thirty years of age, was touring Japan on a preaching mission. Yet it highlights an important facet of Sundar's personality which became apparent early in his ministry. The Japanese girl was not alone in noticing the resemblance between master and servant. In what ways were they similar? To some extent it was a physical likeness, but more important there was in Sundar's personality and life-style much that resembled Jesus Christ.

His pale brown skin, bearded face and simple clothing evoked a striking physical similarity which was underlined by his unassuming confidence.

A close look at Sundar's life reveals further points that correspond with the life of Jesus. Both had denied themselves a home and the comfort and joy of family life. In his role as 'sadhu' Sundar had adopted the same manner of life as Jesus, that of the itinerant evangelist. As Jesus had preached the Gospel to the people of Palestine, using simple language and parables drawn from nature and the everyday lives of his listeners, so Sundar Singh preached to the Indians.

Jesus needed solitude to pray and to commune with his Father. Likewise periods of meditation were essential to Sundar, and the lonely hill of North India and Tibet gave him ample opportunity. Sundar did strive towards *The Imitation of*

Christ and as we have seen this classic of the spiritual life was a book to which he returned time and time again.

Saint Luke begins the fourth chapter of his Gospel with these words:

> Full of the Holy Spirit, Jesus returned from the Jordan, and for forty days was led by the Spirit up and down the wilderness and tempted by the devil.
>
> All that time he had nothing to eat, and at the end of it he was famished. (NEB).

As Sundar read and re-read the Gospel narratives of Our Lord's fasting in the wilderness, an idea took root in his mind. Jesus had entered the solitude to fast and pray as part of his preparation for his public ministry. Sundar regretted that he himself had not done the same. In 1913, eight years after he had first put on his sadhu's robe, he determined to remedy this.

Where should he go? Along the banks of the Ganges between Dehra Dun and Hardwar, the forestation is particularly dense. Only an occasional party of labourers cutting bamboo ever ventured far into the Forest of Kajliban. For the purpose of a retreat this area had obvious attractions.

In January 1913 Sundar was in Central India and he proceeded northwards by train in the direction of Kajliban. The journey took him several days. He did not travel by a direct route since he chose to stop at various points to preach and teach. It was whilst he made his way northwards that he met, in a railway carriage, a Roman Catholic doctor named Smith.

The identity of this man remains a mystery. In some versions of the story his name is given as 'Swift'. Nor is it clear whether he was a medical practitioner or whether he was a doctor in some other field of study.

Sundar revealed his plan to fast for forty days to Dr Smith who tried hard yet unsuccessfully to dissuade him. Before their ways parted Dr Smith insisted that Sundar should give him the names of six close friends. Presumably Dr Smith anticipated that Sundar would not survive the fast and that he would die. Had he waited until news of Sundar's disappearance had been circulated, before he acted, his part in this story would be less puzzling.

For on 22nd January within hours of Dr Smith's parting from Sundar six telegrams were despatched from Nimoda, a small railway station in Central India. They were sent, amongst others, to Dr Wherry, Sundar's headmaster at Ludhiana, to Mr Redman, his friend at Simla who had baptised him, and to Bishop Lefroy. They all bore the same brief message, 'Sundar Singh slept in Christ' and were signed 'Smith'.

The news spread that Sundar Singh was dead. His friends mourned. A memorial service was held at Saint Thomas's Church, Simla. Obituary notices appeared in the newspapers. Plans to erect a memorial were set in motion. However the sole evidence of Sundar's death was a cryptic telegram from an unknown man called Smith. No corpse had been found and Sundar's friends must have hoped for some happier explanation of the telegrams.

Meanwhile Sundar, oblivious of the telegrams' despatch, continued his journey north and eventually reached Kajliban Forest. He made his way into the dense undergrowth until he came to a clearing. Having placed a heap of forty stones beside him, he planned to cast one aside each day until none remained.

His fast began. In the world outside the forest his friends grieved.

Towards the end of February Bishop Lefroy was surprised

to receive a letter from Annfield from Sundar dated 22nd February. He told the Bishop that he had undertaken the forty days' fast, but that his health had broken down and that he had collapsed from exhaustion and exposure. He had been saved by bamboo cutters who, by chance, had stumbled upon his forest hideaway, found him unconscious and carried him to safety.

Probably at the time Sundar wrote that letter he believed he had fasted for forty days, but it is apparent that the length of the fast was nearer twenty days. Sundar later realised that his first assertion that he had been in the Kajliban Forest for the full forty days was mistaken. He agreed that he must have been found comparatively soon after losing consciousness. There was a naïveté in Sundar's make-up that would have assumed that because Jesus had fasted forty days and because he sought to imitate Jesus, that he too would have been led by God to undergo an identical experience.

Bishop Appasamy in his biography maps out the probable sequence of events. It is known for certain that Sundar preached at Indore on 19th January. Indore was some four hundred miles from the Kajliban Forest. From Sundar's own account it appears that he visited other towns and villages on his way to Kajliban, so it is unlikely he reached his destination before 26th or 27th January. Meanwhile he had met Dr Smith and the telegrams had been sent. Sundar's letter to the Bishop was dated 22nd February, twenty-seven days later. This certainly rules out the possibility of a complete forty-day fast and indicates that it probably lasted about three weeks.

The telegrams remain an unsolved mystery. Attempts to trace Dr Smith were unsuccessful. It can only be assumed that he was so certain that Sundar intended to undertake the fast, and equally certain that he would die in the attempt, that he sent the telegrams as soon as he parted from Sundar. The latter was still travelling to Kajliban when his six friends received their telegrams. Had he delayed his fast a little longer he might well have heard the rumours of his own death. As it was he disappeared into the forest for three weeks knowing nothing whatever of the turmoil and grief his absence was causing.

Setting aside the question of when and for how long he fasted, of what further importance is this experience? Sundar's own words in *A Collection of Incidents* indicate both his motive for undertaking the fast and the benefits he derived from it.

> After several years of service I felt guided to go into some forest where, free from any kind of interruption, I could have a forty days' fast and ask for blessing on past work and for power for the future. When I first commenced the fast, for several days I experienced great hardship. Afterwards it was not at all difficult.
>
> But the blood dried up to such an extent that I altogether lost the power of sight and speech. I could hear nothing and by reason of weakness could not even turn myself. But certainly my intellectual powers were sharpened several times over, from which I gathered proof of the true fact that the soul is an entity that cannot cease to exist when the body dies, but goes on living. In that condition I experienced the Presence of God and the fullness of the Spirit, which cannot be expressed in words. In that condition too I had a vision of the Lord in a glorious form, from which I gained the conviction that now He would assuredly keep me alive to serve Him for some time.

Sundar further elaborated on his experience in the forest when, in 1920, he visited Oxford. Bishop Appasamy, then a student, and Canon B. H. Streeter, an Oxford theologian, were gathering material for a book they wrote jointly called *The*

Sadhu. It was a study of Sundar's spiritual life and was published in 1921.

He recalled to them that his feeling of peace was so overpowering that he felt no temptation to abandon the fast, but immersed himself gladly in a tide of joy.

Sundar was able to pinpoint unmistakable benefits that he attributed to the fast. He regarded it as an important stride along the road of his discipleship. Firstly it confirmed his belief that the peace and joy he experienced came from God and were not due to some capacity of his own spirit. In other words the spirit was different from the brain. "The brain," he said, in an attempt to express this idea pictorially, "is only the office where the spirit works."

Secondly from that time onwards he felt better able to combat temptations to abandon his life as a sadhu with its continual hardships. Thirdly he was less irritated after this experience by the questions he was continually subjected to from curious listeners.

Although, as we have seen, the fast lasted considerably less than the planned forty days, it is certain that he was in a very weak condition when the bamboo cutters found him and that he only survived as a result of their timely intervention.

They carried him out of the forest and from there to the Christian community at Annfield. No doubt they decided to take him there after finding a copy of the New Testament by his side.

At Annfield he was taken to the home of the Reverend Dharamjit Singh. Unfortunately Dharamjit Singh was away from home, but his adopted son Bansi agreed to take Sundar in and cared for him until the pastor returned. Bansi nursed him capably and fed him on liquids until his strength began to increase. It was three weeks before he was well enough to leave Annfield. His body bore the marks of the privations he had imposed upon it, yet he was full of plans to resume afresh his work for his Master.

On 16th March 1913 he visited Thomas Riddle at Nahan who noted in his diary, "Sundar Singh again arrived: now going to the Tibet border." Thomas Riddle recalled this visit in his articles on Sundar, and in July 1946 he recorded in *The United Church Review* that Sundar looked pale and worn.

March, April, May—the snows began to melt and swell the rivers, and for Sundar, Tibet beckoned again. His experiences in the Kajliban Forest had confirmed him in his determination to serve his Lord and to tell others of his Master's love for mankind. In Tibet in the summer of 1913 Sundar was going to need all the spiritual resources he could muster.

Preaching in Tibet had always been hard, had always been dangerous, but on this particular expedition everything seemed to be against him. The people were more hostile than ever, which meant food was harder to come by. His physique had not wholly recovered from the effects of the fast earlier in the year. Further demands through hunger, cold and sheer physical exhaustion became his daily portion, yet he was undaunted. He would not turn back as long as the weather permitted him to stay. Once the snows came travel would be impossible and he was determined to grasp every opportunity to proclaim his faith.

Eventually he came to Rasar and began preaching in the market place. A small crowd gathered to listen and showed a cautious interest in his words. Sundar was encouraged to continue. Suddenly the mood of the crowd changed. Some slipped quietly away. Others became belligerent and Sundar had to face a torrent of abuse and threatening gestures. At first he was at a loss to understand the change in their manner. The reason soon became apparent. The people were being provoked by the servants of the Grand Lama. Once it was known that the lama disapproved of the young man in the yellow robe, all interest in Sundar's preaching evaporated. To his dismay Sundar saw monastery guards advancing across the market place towards him. Without ceremony he was arrested and dragged into the monastery and brought before the Grand Lama.

Sundar knew he could expect no mercy. It was forbidden to preach a foreign religion in Tibet and the Grand Lama was obviously relishing his right to enforce the law. Sundar could offer no defence nor did he wish to excuse himself or deny his message. His punishment was death. His captors did not intend to kill him outright. Such an act was against their Buddhist principles. However they were prepared to punish their captives in a manner that would cause death, cruel though this was.

Sundar was dragged outside to a dry well beyond the town. The lid was removed and Sundar was thrown in. He fell many feet to the bottom. Above him the well cover was locked firmly into place and the key, the only key, was returned to the Grand Lama. The fetid stench at the foot of the well was unbelievable, and although mercifully it was too dark to see, Sundar knew that he was surrounded by the rotting corpses of previous prisoners. He had fallen awkwardly and the acute pain in his arm indicated that it had been broken.

The situation seemed utterly lost. He felt that he could have faced almost any death rather than this slow torture. He prayed that God would save him but he prayed more in faith than in hope. The putrid air, the lack of water and food, and the interminable darkness wore down his spirit hour by hour.

Three days passed. All Sundar now hoped for was the quick release of death and for this he prepared. His prayers that night were interrupted by a grinding noise above. A key rasped in a lock. As he struggled to his feet he could feel the fresh air blowing down the well. The lid had been opened and in the moonlight he saw a rope swinging beside him. The end was tied in a loop. One of his arms was useless and he was weak from lack of food. Mustering his strength he placed one leg through the loop and clung on with his good arm as the rope was pulled up from the top. He felt his body being lifted over the rim of the well and laid gently on the ground. He lay there weakly listening to the sound of the well-cover being replaced. Every minute in the fresh air restored him and he raised himself a little to thank his rescuers. They had already gone. Sundar struggled to his feet and looked around. He was quite alone.

In the early morning Sundar, refreshed by a night's sleep, washed out his sadhu's robe and laid it to dry. He debated what to do. It was tempting to thank God for his deliverance and to leave Rasar as fast as possible. Yet the more he pondered the situation the more he felt that he would be wasting an opportunity if he crept out of the town unnoticed. What had God saved him for?

By midday Sundar was back in the market place preaching to a wide-eyed and incredulous crowd. The news that he had escaped from the well, spread through the town and reached the ears of the Grand Lama. Once more Sundar was arrested and brought before him.

Someone in Rasar had rescued the Christian by stealing the key and that person was a traitor. The Grand Lama was anxious to find him. Sundar was questioned closely, but he could not explain his rescue any more than the lama could. How could anyone have stolen the key from the lama's belt? Sundar did not know.

The lama fingered the keys at his waist. The interrogation ceased abruptly. The key to the well was still there. He stared at Sundar, the terror apparent in his eyes.

"Get out of this place," he cried. "Never return here, lest the power that protects you, should bring disaster upon us."

The people cowered back in silence to let Sundar pass. He left Rasar and no one tried to stop him.

Rasar has never been identified on any map of Tibet. We have only Sundar's word for the story. His detractors maintained that he had fabricated the incident. There is certainly no proof that it occurred. There is no proof that it didn't. There is however the unwavering conviction amongst his friends that he was an entirely honest man and that such a deliberate lie would be so out of character as to make nonsense of his whole life.

The beginning of 1913 had found Sundar preaching in Central India just before his fast. His ministry which had begun in the villages of North India was being extended to other parts of the country. He was becoming a well-known figure. In general among his fellow Christians his name was mentioned in tones of respect and enthusiasm. Many appreciated the vision of the Christian life that he presented to India. Understandably, however, there were those who regarded him with the mistrust which frequently attaches to pioneers in any field. The fact that he sat lightly to the institutional church was resented. Others, with far less justification, were jealous of his abilities and sought opportunity to denigrate him. His vagueness and disregard for details of place and date and his carefree and uninhibited retelling of his spiritual experiences served to make him a sitting target for attack. Since he was not concerned with establishing his own reputation he did not bother to defend himself.

In 1913 these criticisms only amounted to murmurs. They were however to grow in volume and were eventually to reach crescendo heights. In 1913 Sundar was still unperturbed. Opposition did not frighten him and for him 1913 stood out because it was the year of his fast, a milestone in his discipleship.

Already he was reaping the benefits of this undertaking. For according to his friend, Thomas Riddle, it was during this year that he began to have visionary experiences when he was praying. These he regarded as an unmerited gift from God, a bonus bestowed on some yet withheld from others. He accepted these manifestations of God's grace with humility and gratitude, as outward and visible signs of a Divine Love both enduring and boundless.

7

> Thereafter the day shall come when I will pour out my spirit on all mankind; your sons and your daughters shall prophesy, your old men shall dream dreams and your young men see visions. (Joel 2 : 28 NEB).

"YOUR YOUNG MEN shall see visions." This was God's promise recorded by the prophet Joel, a promise that was to be gloriously fulfilled not only on the Day of Pentecost but also in the experience of Christians throughout the centuries. How aptly these words apply to Sundar Singh. The ecstatic experiences that were to occur in Sundar's life with increasing frequency came not only when he was at prayer, but also in the midst of turmoil and dangers of his life. Unbidden and unheralded, these assurances of God's continuing presence were, time and again, to uphold him, sometimes in unexpected circumstances.

In June 1914 Sundar was travelling between villages on the borders of Nepal during a storm. A sudden gust of wind hurled him into a hollow in the rocks, and in the midst of his frustration at being forced to shelter he was shown in a vision scenes from the Passion of Christ. When he saw with renewed clarity what his Lord had endured Sundar felt his own hardships had been negligible by comparison and he felt encouraged despite the current difficulties of preaching in Nepal.

There were indeed great difficulties. At that time foreign missionaries were as unpopular in Nepal as in Tibet. Added to that the terrain itself was similarly rugged and inhospitable.

Shortly after Sundar's visionary experience by the rock, he arrived at Ilam, one of the larger Nepalese towns. He described his reception at Ilam in a letter to the journal *Nur Afshan.* This was a Christian publication in Urdu for which Sundar wrote a series of letters between 1912 and 1917 describing his work. This account appeared on 3rd July 1914, a month after his arrival:

> The day I reached Ilam was a special day in which the bazaars were full, like a market day. I began preaching, standing in the bazaar before the post-office. The people gathered together in a large number . . . Many heard me attentively and I distributed Gospels which were in the vernacular of Nepal. During this time the official got the news. He became very angry and asked who had given me permission to enter Nepal and preach.

Sundar continues his letter with a detailed record of the conversation he had with this official, whom he called 'Officer' and whose precise title is unclear. He explained his presence in Nepal to his interrogator in these terms: "Because God through Christ has called all nations to life eternal and when I came to know that Nepal is unaware of this fact He ordered me to give you this Gospel."

Sundar was unimpressed by threats of imprisonment, and in his account of this episode in *Nur Afshan* he gives the impression that the Nepalese decided that the simplest course would be to expel him from the country. They feared he would influence the other prisoners and so sent him under armed escort to the border.

There was however an important sequel to this story which Sundar omitted to mention in *Nur Afshan.* Six months later when Sundar came to write his Urdu book *A Collection of Incidents* which has already been mentioned, Sundar described how he had been imprisoned at Ilam. We can only assume that he returned to Ilam soon after his first expulsion.

Incensed at his persistence the authorities decided to deter this obstinate offender for good. The prison was in the centre of Ilam and in its yard and in sight of the gaping crowd, Sundar was stripped of his clothes and put into stocks. Leeches were placed close to him and everyone watched as they began to crawl over his body and suck his blood. Sundar wrote, "For two or three hours I felt my sufferings very much indeed, but afterwards my Lord by His Holy Presence turned my prison into a paradise."

It was this strange unexpected surge of joy in the middle of great physical pain that prompted Sundar to rejoice openly and sing. The crowd outside swelled as more and more citizens gathered to watch and listen. Sundar soon had a sizeable audience and he therefore began to preach. The atmosphere was electric. Everyone listened to his voice. They could not but be moved by the sight of this man, his body in agony, yet his face and voice radiating joy. They could not but wonder at the power his religion gave him.

This was not to the liking of the Nepalese officials and they made a fresh decision to release Sundar and ban him for ever from Nepal. They too wondered at the power that sustained him. Fearful of that power, they were anxious to be rid of him.

Again there are variations in the story. Sundar's account in *A Collection of Incidents* gives the impression that he was able to walk away after he was released, although he does mention that loss of blood caused him to feel dizzy. Perhaps Sundar himself was anxious to play down the more sensational aspects of the episode when he wrote *A Collection of Incidents*, just as for the wider readership of *Nur Afshan* he had entirely omitted any allusion to his imprisonment. Mrs Rebecca

Parker, a personal friend and admirer of Sundar Singh wrote in 1918 the book *Sadhu Sundar Singh—Called of God* deriving her material from conversations with Sundar. In describing the events at Ilam and in particular Sundar's condition after being released from the stocks she wrote:

> This dreadful experience had made him so weak that he fell unconscious, and only after some time and many attempts did he manage to crawl away from the spot. In that place were some secret believers belonging to the Sannyasi Mission and these kind people received their wounded brother and cared for him until strength returned.

Sundar was asked why he had not mentioned his imprisonment and punishment at Ilam in his letter to the journal *Nur Afshan*. He cited these two reasons. He felt a certain modesty and had no wish to dwell on his privations. Secondly he was a British subject. Any inquiry in government circles about his treatment in Nepal would draw attention to the incident, and such unwelcome publicity might prompt the Nepalese to tighten security, and thus reduce still further the chances of a missionary gaining entry.

At the time he confided the story to the Parkers, the question of Mrs Rebecca Parker writing a book about him had not yet arisen, so he was not inhibited by the thought of publicity. However when she began the book she naturally recalled the version she had heard from Sundar himself.

These discrepancies are not outright contradictions; it is simply that some versions omit sections of the story prominent in others.

Sundar's critics were later to seize upon the divergent reports to support their contention that Sundar was a fraud. The fact that there is no mention in official records at Ilam of the imprisonment is admittedly puzzling. Two facts should perhaps be borne in mind when we read of this incident.

First there is the inscription on the flyleaf of Sundar's New Testament written in his own handwriting and seen by Rebecca Parker: "Nepal. 7 June 1914. Christ's presence has turned my prison into a blessed heaven; what then will it do in heaven hereafter?"

Secondly there is the evidence of a young Tibetan Christian named Tharchin whom Sundar had helped in 1908. On that occasion he had recognised Tharchin as the former servant of one of the Moravian missionaries. Tharchin was down on his luck and Sundar had suggested that he should come and live with him. Sundar at that time had temporary lodgings with the Church Missionary Society in Simla. Work was found for Tharchin and a close relationship was formed between the two. Sundar's influence on Tharchin was to set the latter on a path of Christian service that eventually culminated in his ordination as a minister in the Church of North India.

Tharchin recorded in his diary in the first half of June 1914 that Sundar visited him at his home near Darjeeling. Sundar's body was covered with sores which Tharchin treated with iodine. These sores could well have been caused by his ill-treatment in the Ilam prison. Darjeeling was less than fifty miles east of Ilam over the border into India.

Sundar was sufficiently recovered by 17th June for Tharchin and himself to consider a joint evangelistic venture.

"Let's go to Tibet together," suggested Sundar. "We can try a new route. We will go north from here and approach Tibet through Sikkhim." Tharchin agreed with this plan and they prepared for their journey.

However their plans were frustrated by red tape for they failed to get a permit to travel beyond Gangtok, the capital of the State of Sikkhim. As a route into Tibet it was obviously not satisfactory. Sundar and Tharchin returned to India. It was too late in the year to approach Tibet any other way so Sundar returned to Kotgarh, grateful no doubt for an unexpected opportunity for rest and solitude. Samuel Stokes, now married, had a house four miles outside Kotgarh. While he and his wife were in America, Sundar had the run of the house.

For several months he divided his time three ways—preaching in the surrounding villages, talking to the students of Saint Stephen's College, Delhi (where his friend Susil Rudra was Principal), who were in Kotgarh for their vacation, and refreshing his own spirit by prayer and meditation.

This allocation of his time symbolises the balance of Sundar's Christian commitment. He was not a solitary mystic, a maharishi isolated from the world, but an active servant of God. When Bishop Appasamy and Canon Streeter were assembling material for their book on the mystical aspect of Sundar's life they put to him this question: "If you had a week all to yourself, what would you do with it? Would you spend it in prayer or in active evangelism?" Sundar replied: "Can we drink only water or eat only food for a week? We require both drink and food."

This is not an original view of the Christian life, indeed Our Lord himself in his public ministry kept such a balance, but the degree to which Sundar developed both his interior life of prayer and his outgoing life of service was exceptional. Lives such as Sundar Singh's bridge the division between the East and West in the mingling of these two facets of the Christian discipline—the way of service and the way of prayer. Sundar, neither hermit nor humanist, expressed in his life of service sustained by prayer, a synthesis which would be hard to emulate.

Talking of the place of prayer in the life of a Christian,

Sundar Singh said, "Once I was sitting on the bank of a river and observed some fish coming up to the surface and opening their mouths. I thought they wanted to eat the smaller fish. But an expert in these matters afterwards told me that they had to come up to the surface occasionally for air even though they could breathe to a certain extent under water. Like these fish, Christians also have to rise from time to time above their daily occupations in order that they may come into closer contact with God, even though while occupied in their work they can keep in touch with Him."

Sundar spoke from his own experience for this was how he himself felt the need to pray in the midst of a life of service. For what other purpose did he pray? Did he seek to persuade a reluctant God, to effect a change of heart in the Divine? This puzzling question as to the purpose of prayer which has always exercised Christians, Sundar was to answer explicitly in his book *Reality and Religion* (1923). He wrote:

> By prayer we cannot change God's plans, as some people seem to think. But the man who prays is himself changed. The capacities of the soul, which are imperfect in this imperfect life, are daily reaching towards perfection.
>
> A bird sits brooding over her eggs. At first, in the eggs, there is only a kind of liquid without form or shape. As the mother continues to sit on them, the unformed matter in the eggs becomes changed into the form of the mother. The change is not in the mother but in the eggs. So, when we pray, God is not changed but we are changed into His glorious image and likeness.

Here we have a glimpse into Sundar's theology of prayer. How did he translate this into daily practice? Appasamy and Streeter questioned Sundar on this point. He stated that the varying circumstances of his life prevented him from following an unchanging and inflexible routine. On some days he was able to set aside three or four hours, on others considerably less. The bedrock of his prayer was a passage of Scripture, which formed the starting point of his meditation and was followed by a time of recollection.

Sundar explained that the Holy Spirit taught him what to pray for both in regard to others and in regard to himself. Intercession, rooted in the down-to-earth practicalities of sickness, ignorance or unbelief was a constant obligation. He preferred solitude and needed silence.

The quiet undramatic life at Kotgarh in the summer of 1914 gave way to the more strenuous pattern of life of the itinerant evangelist. India in the winter, Tibet in the summer. The routine was becoming established. This was Sundar's life for the next three years.

Here is an extract from a letter which he received from his father in 1916. It reminds us that the old resentments still lingered on. Sher Singh wrote:

> My dear son, light of my eyes, comfort of my life, may you live long! You have not replied to the message which I sent to you through the tailor Dasundhi. Now I do not ask for your opinion but order you to marry soon. Does the Christian religion teach that you should not obey your parents? Can you not serve your Guru Christ after you are married? Think a little. Who will take care of the house and property? Will you efface the name of the family? If you agree to your betrothal today, I will give in your charge a sum of money the monthly interest of which will be about Rs. 300/-. Otherwise whatever stands in your name, don't hope for it. Your affectionate father, SHER SINGH.

Ten years had elapsed since Sundar had left his father's house in Rampur, and still his father seemed to have little or no understanding of the faith that motivated Sundar. He wrote to the twenty-six-year-old son with the same extravagant mixture of bribes and threats that he had used to bully the sixteen-year-old rebel.

Marriage was out of the question for Sundar, although he had none of the Hindu ascetic's suspicion of women. The respect in which he held his mother would not have permitted that. His relationships with women, like his relationships with children, were easy and relaxed. His nomadic life, however, ruled out by definition the possibility of a stable home and marriage. Since he had chosen this particular service of the Lord, he could not also fulfil the obligations of marriage and parenthood, if he was to remain faithful to his vocation.

Courteously but firmly he wrote to his father regretting that he was unable to comply with his father's bidding on the subject of marriage. Sundar was mildly surprised by his father's declared intention to cut him out of his Will since he had been under the impression that his father had done just that ten years earlier.

In 1916 during his summer visit to Tibet, Sundar met once again the Maharishi of Kailash. The journal *Nur Afshan* published his detailed account of their joint conversations and speculation in this strange hermit flared up again. Sundar was anxious that others should accompany him to Kailash, and see for themselves that the Maharishi existed. Consequently on 25th January 1917 Sundar invited through the columns of *Nur Afshan* anyone who wished to undertake the journey to make ready. He emphasised the difficulties involved and gave the address of a friend through whom prospective participants could reach him.

On 4th April 1917 Sundar left Dehra Dun for Tibet with

four companions. Their destination was Kailash. Mussoorie was to be their first stop, barely ten miles north of Dehra Dun. At Mussoorie one of the four, already exhausted by the rigours of travelling over that terrain, regretfully dropped out from the expedition. Another of the travellers followed suit and Sundar was left with only two companions, Mr A. S. Judson, a teacher, and Mr B. Mohan Lal, a Quaker.

Sundar chose the route via Gangotri, which although arduous was frequently used by travellers. The enthusiasm of Mr Judson and Mr Mohan Lal was dampened by a period of stormy weather. Both of them suffered from dysentery and fever. Sundar had perhaps been unrealistic to expect them to withstand the austerities of the journey. His body was hardened to the rigours of walking mile after mile in rough country, and he himself was able to do so lightly clad and with a meagre supply of food. His companions were not at the same peak of physical fitness.

Severe snowstorms finally forced them to abandon their goal and they had to retrace their steps. Mr Judson was particularly disappointed in their failure to reach Kailash. Sundar suggested that the two of them should attempt to enter Tibet by another route, but Mr Judson, having already lost part of his luggage, decided that he should return with Mohan Lal to Mussoorie.

Sundar bade his friends farewell. He was saddened that the expedition should have proved so abortive, but determined nevertheless that he himself would press on. His persistence was rewarded. He did visit the Maharishi that summer for the third and last time, and as it turned out, he was not alone.

Not far from Kailash he met a Tibetan lama called Fangche with whom he fell into conversation. Lama Fangche asked Sundar if they might travel together to the Maharishi. Two days later they reached their destination.

Sundar was to write a detailed account of their conversation with the Maharishi for *Nur Afshan* on 27th July 1917, a few weeks after the meeting.

The Maharishi, Sundar reported, began their conversation by referring to Sundar's four fellow-travellers who had failed to complete the journey. It appeared to Sundar that the Maharishi had such powers of vision and perception that he had been able to follow the progress of their journey.

"It does not matter," said the Maharishi, "that I am physically living at a great distance. Our dear Lord is always near us all. It is far better for them (he referred to Sundar's four companions) to pray and obtain his grace. I will also add my prayers to theirs, and beg that their service may bear fruit. Tell them to give up the desire of getting higher pay and to keep themselves engaged in the service of the Lord; if they do so they will get everything."

The rest of the conversation dealt with the origins of Christianity in India. It has already been noted that Mrs Rebecca Parker in her account of Sundar's imprisonment at Ilam, said that Sundar, after his release, was cared for by 'some secret believers belonging to the Sannyasi Mission'. Both the Maharishi and Sundar were aware of the existence of this group, and the Maharishi told Sundar that he regarded himself as a member of the Mission.

The Mission traced its origins to the evangelistic endeavours of the Apostle Thomas who by tradition first brought the Gospel to India. The history of the Sannyasi Mission is hard to uncover. It seems to have been a small flame flickering through centuries of Indian history, never quite extinguished, never a roaring fire. At the beginning of this century its members were mainly high caste Hindu converts. They met regularly in churches that looked like Hindu temples. Their simple services consisted mainly of Bible study, although baptism and

Holy Communion were regularly celebrated. Their password was '*Yisu Nasrinâth kî jai*'—'Victory belongs to Jesus of Nazareth'.

Sundar had found their reticence puzzling and had urged them to declare their faith more boldly. Their reply was that they preferred to proceed like fishermen who unobtrusively fill their nets with fish. When their nets were full they would then declare their presence to the world, a presence which by this time had reached out from India to include Tibet and Nepal. It is therefore a possibility that members of the Mission, who may have lain undetected for years at Rasar, did play some part in Sundar's release from the well.

When Sundar, in the course of his conversation with the Maharishi, remarked that many people had doubts about the existence of the Sannyasi Mission, the Maharishi brushed this aside. He urged Sundar not to worry if people disbelieved him. Here the Maharishi was referring to an article by a Dr Dutta, which had appeared in *Nur Afshan*, in which the writer claimed that Sundar's meetings with the Maharishi were not authentic but the product of a vivid imagination. The Maharishi was aware of the reservations in people's minds when Sundar mentioned their meetings, yet insisted that Sundar must not be disturbed when people doubted or misunderstood. Sundar's task was to proceed with his work. Encouraged by this conversation with the Maharishi, Sundar determined to do just that.

Whether we consider Dr Dutta to have made a reasonable point or not, this was sound advice in view of the ever-growing censure with which Sundar was confronted.

Not all Sundar's experiences invited incredulity or raised questions about his veracity. It may have been on this journey in Tibet that one of the most notable and most renowned of all

Sundar's adventures occurred. Moreover, it proved to be one which no one later felt moved to doubt.

Sundar was caught, while travelling over a mountain range, by a sudden heavy snowstorm. The temperature dropped rapidly but there was nowhere to shelter, so he trudged on. He was heartened to hear a shout. Coming up behind him was a Tibetan anxious for his company. The two men struggled on together, their steps slow and laboured. The same insistent question was in the minds of each of them. How long could their bodies survive the savage bitter wind?

Momentarily the snowfall ceased and with the improved visibility they were able to see that their path skirted a thirty-foot drop down to a rocky ledge. Sundar could just make out a dark form lying inert on the ledge below. Marks where the snow had been disturbed on the bank confirmed his suspicions. Clearly a traveller had fallen down the steep slope.

"Look, there's a man down there. We must climb down and help him up if he's still alive," Sundar told his companion.

"Are you mad?" asked the Tibetan incredulously. "We shall all three perish unless we get to the next village without delay. Leave him for dead and perhaps we two will survive."

Sundar pleaded but the man was adamant.

"You may risk your life if you wish, but I am going on." Sundar watched the retreating figure for a moment, and then began his cautious descent towards the crumpled form below him. As he had feared the man was unconscious. Slowly Sundar dragged him up to the path. He could not rest for long in that icy atmosphere, and he knew he must get the man to a warm shelter before nightfall.

Sundar bent down and with a mighty effort hoisted the man over his shoulders. He staggered forward awkwardly and then somehow managed to settle into an even pace. He could not move fast but at least he kept moving, pausing only for the briefest stops. As he rounded a corner later in the day he saw his former Tibetan companion sitting it seemed in the snow. Sundar called out to him. There was no reply. The man was dead, frozen stiff by the bitter cold. Sundar pressed on subdued by the macabre sight he had just witnessed.

Just before he reached the safety of a village, Sundar felt the dead weight of the man on his shoulders stir slightly. He himself no longer felt cold. The friction of their two bodies and Sundar's own exertions had warmed them and kept both alive. Sundar by endangering his life to save another had unknowingly preserved his own. As they passed the first dwelling house the man regained consciousness and with Sundar's help was able to walk. Sheltering that night in warmth and safety they were both full of thankfulness to be alive.

8

DECEMBER 1917:

At Ratnagiri a special meeting was arranged for the lawyers in the town. They came with their families. There must have been about two hundred people present. After the meeting three lawyers prostrated themselves before him. The Sadhu said, "Don't do this," and lifted them up. The women crowded round him, took hold of his scarf and put it on the heads of their children. They would also touch his garment reverently.

In these words to Bishop Appasamy a young Indian Christian, Vincent David, who was accompanying the Sadhu, recalled Sundar's preaching tour of West India in the final months of 1917.

". . . a special meeting was arranged for lawyers in the town . . . they would also touch his garment reverently." Two fresh factors in Sundar's ministry were becoming apparent. His work now embraced a wider public. Gone were the days when Sundar could wander from one village to another at will and talk with whoever came his way. That spontaneous and informal approach had given place to organised tours with pre-arranged programmes and carefully timed schedules. The publicity which now preceded him ensured that everywhere he went a sizeable audience would gather to await his arrival.

Between the large public meetings he was determined to continue that person-to-person ministry that he had so successfully exercised in earlier years. Sundar, like his Lord, never lost touch with individuals.

This development, with its emphasis on the public image of Sundar Singh, brings us to the second new feature of his work. Like all popular figures, his name and reputation were becoming legendary. Vincent David's report of lawyers who prostrated themselves and women who touched his clothes gives us a graphic picture of the new role in which Sundar found himself cast. It was a potentially dangerous one, not because Sundar was likely to have his head turned by mass adulation, but because it indicated in his listeners' minds a confusion between the Master and the servant. There was a risk that the preaching was being obscured by the preacher, or, as we would say today, the message by the medium. Sundar was himself aware of the dangers. So were others, particularly European missionaries who feared for his integrity.

It was at this stage that Sundar's powers of oratory came into full play. His mental and physical stamina, his unyielding faith and tender compassion had long been evident; now he revealed a remarkable and innate ability to speak in public. For many Indians it was the first time they had heard the Gospel from a fellow-Indian. This fact, allied with Sundar's fluency and persuasiveness of speech, made a powerful impact on people who had hitherto, consciously or unconsciously, associated Christianity with a white face, the British Raj and European dress.

At Poona, Sundar visited the Mission House run by the Anglican community, known as the Society of Saint John the Evangelist. Reports of Sundar's presence amongst them came back to England, to the mother house of the order at Cowley, Oxford. In the March 1918 edition of the Society's periodical *The Cowley Evangelist*, Sister Amy Sybilla, on the staff of the Mission in Poona, wrote a long account of Sundar's visit and the effect his preaching had on the girls in their charge. "One of our girls remarked to a Sister, 'Yes, we have heard all this from you, Sister, many times before, but to think that one of our own people is speaking like that and praying like that, is wonderful.' "

Similar sentiments were echoed by a Hindu who had attended an open-air rally at Kolhapur, addressed by Sundar, at which three hundred people had been present. This Hindu was one of some twelve converts who, after hearing Sundar speak, had decided to ask for baptism. Testifying on behalf of his friends he said, "We are willing to accept Christ; we knew all about Christ for the last twenty years from the European missionaries; but now we understand truly that he is the only Saviour."

Sundar was thus realising Bishop Lefroy's hopes for him. He was giving to the people of India a vision, an ideal of what Indian Christianity should and could be.

The problem for Sundar himself at this stage in his work was to continue this public ministry without compromising the way of life he had undertaken on becoming a sadhu. In many ways that mode of life was becoming impractical, inappropriate to the life of a public speaker, much in demand. The claims of diary and timetable had to be respected. Sundar could have been excused for adjusting his life-style to the new opportunities that lay before him. To his credit he did not do so. He took the harder course of remaining faithful to his original vocation whilst at the same time meeting the new challenge.

Central to his original vocation had been the life of poverty. Apart from his sadhu's robe and turban, a blanket and New Testament, he had no possessions. From now on he had to fight to keep it that way. Grateful and admiring listeners pressed upon him presents and money. It was hard to refuse without giving offence. Again Vincent David's reminiscences to Bishop Appasamy highlight this difficulty. "Sundar Singh was invited (at Kolhapur) to go and listen to the boarders in a Girls' Hostel singing Christian lyrics on three successive nights in the open air. He was clad in his usual saffron robe. It was quite cold and he wrapped around himself on the first night the cotton scarf which he generally wore over his robe. The girls, who observed this, collected some money and gave him a warm and expensive shawl on the second night. He accepted the gift gratefully and used it that night as well as on the following night. On the third evening as we were returning home from the meeting we saw an old man in tattered clothes under a tree seeking to warm himself before a fire. The sadhu took off his shawl, wrapped it round the old man and walked away."

Until now in his ministry Sundar had travelled mainly on foot. The demands of time and the long distances he was required to travel meant that journeys by rail were essential. Sundar conceded that this was necessary and gratefully accepted from his hosts a rail ticket to his next destination. However it was his custom to refuse absolutely any other expenses. Vincent David recalled how on one occasion an envelope containing money was thrust at Sundar as the train drew out of Kadoli Station. It was not long in Sundar's possession. By the time the train reached Bangalore he was empty-handed and a beggar at an intermediate station was rejoicing in his good fortune.

When he had been a little-known itinerant preacher in the villages of North India and Tibet, Sundar had been able to order his routine much as he chose. Travel on foot ensured that the pace of life was relatively slow. He had been able to offer to God regular and ample time for prayer and meditation, since communion with God was, for Sundar, as essential as breathing. Now others arranged his daily programme. So enthusiastic were they to give as many people as possible the chance to hear

Sundar Singh that they packed his day with one engagement after another.

Sundar could not hope to carry out such an arduous time-table without plentiful time for prayer. This was the mainspring of his being and without it he would be an empty shell. So he insisted that, included in any programme, there should be days free of engagements when spiritual and physical recuperation would be possible. He would sacrifice his sleep to make time for prayer. Vincent David found Sundar praying at three in the morning and asked him the next day why he needed so much time for prayer.

Sundar replied, "It takes fifteen to twenty minutes for me to concentrate. Then I begin to pray but I do not use any words. I feel my beloved Jesus so close to me that I place my hands in His. When morning comes and I have to leave my prayer, it is an effort to break away from my Beloved."

The problems that had marked his tour of West India—the over-enthusiastic adulation, the crowded day and the conflict of this new style of life with his vocation as a sadhu—these problems were to remain with Sundar during the years of his public ministry.

They were certainly apparent on his tour of South India which he began in January 1918, immediately after his programme in West India. Christians in South India like those in the North represented a very small minority of the population. However the Church in South India was more firmly established and enjoyed a security unknown to the Christians of the North.

The history of the Church in South India dates back to the third century or earlier. Tradition says that in AD 345 a Syrian Christian trader, Thomas of Cana, came with fellow-Syrians to settle at Malabar, thus beginning the long and complex history of the Syrian Church in South India.

This was the community that welcomed Sundar Singh in 1918—an established church with centuries of Indian history behind it—quite different in character from the Northern Church with its pronounced European bias. There were, of course, European missionaries in the South, who worked in co-operation with the existing church. The Reverend Arthur Parker was a London Missionary Society minister in Trivandram, Travancore, and it was with Mr and Mrs Parker that Sundar stayed for part of his tour. Rebecca Parker was later that year to write a life of Sundar Singh and she records in the Introduction the impact Sundar's visit had on the local community.

She wrote:

> February, 1918, is a time that will linger in the memory of Christians of all denominations in Trivandram, for the visit of Sadhu Sundar Singh was an unprecedented event that brought to many profound spiritual blessing. One of our missionaries rightly said, "Such a figure has never passed through the Indian Church before"; and in passing he left the deep consciousness that God had visited His people.

Numerous incidents from his stay with the Parkers have a New Testament ring about them. A sick man was brought by friends from a village seven miles away to an open-air meeting. A Hindu knocked at the door quietly one evening, anxious to speak to Sundar, just as Nicodemus had once come to Jesus by night.

During this period, as Sundar's fame and reputation increased, so people's expectations of him rose. They believed that he, like Jesus, would heal the sick, and he found it very hard to convince them otherwise. Later in his tour, when it became apparent that he did have healing powers, he felt it necessary to decide once and for all what part this gift should play in his ministry.

His visit to South India coincided with the season of the Christian Conventions. These were annual assemblies of various sections of the Syrian Church, and they normally extended over a period of seven days. It was not unusual for as many as 20,000 Christians to meet together at a Convention. In February 1918, when Sundar was billed as a speaker at a convention in North Travancore, there were no fewer than 32,000 present.

We are indebted to Rebecca Parker for her graphic account of the occasion.

> A rough platform about eighteen inches high had been placed about a third of the way from the back of the booth, and on one end stood two chairs occupied by the two Bishops of the Mar Thoma Syrian Church, who appeared daily in resplendent robes of red or purple satin with gold belts and quaint head-dresses. On the platform below, sitting tailor fashion, were the clergy of the Church, and in front of them in the same lowly style sat the Sadhu.
>
> The vast crowds were seated on the sand, the women all in white on the left, and the men in front and at the right. Away over the sea of heads one caught glimpses of the shining river, with its strange craft plying up and down. A more devout crowd it is not possible to imagine. Every day the early part of the meetings was given to prayer. Subjects were given for silent prayer from time to time by the presiding Bishop, when every head was bowed, and the almost inaudible murmur of prayer gradually increased until a sound like the surging sea rolling in full tide rose all around, a most impressive experience!

The moment came for Sundar to preach. The crowd fell silent, and Sundar rose. He had never before seen Christians in such numbers. Why had this long-established indigenous Church done so little to evangelise their fellow-countrymen in the rest of India? He told the crowd that their neglect had led God to send Americans and Englishmen to North India with the Gospel. He was aware that the leaders of the Syrian Church were awakening to this great challenge, and that a reform movement within the Church was under way. He exhorted them to respond and to share the Gospel far and wide with their brother Indians.

Another aspect of the life of the South Indian Church disturbed Sundar and he drew his audience's attention to it. "A great disability in your Christian witness is your continued recognition of caste divisions. Caste distinction indicates a lack of love and is a disease which cripples the Church and hinders its work."

Sundar's engagements in South India continued until April. He had been touring with hardly a break for six months, first in West India and then in the South. An exhausting programme had been made more arduous by the South's stifling heat, to which Sundar was totally unaccustomed.

Thus it was that in April, Bishop Appasamy's father, Dewan Bahadur Appasamy, invited Sundar to his home at Shenbaganur for rest. Shenbaganur, three miles from Kodaikanal, in the cool of the Palni Hills, was an ideal retreat and Sundar gratefully accepted. A. J. Appasamy was himself away in America reading theology, and was not to meet Sundar on this occasion. His father and brother later provided him with a detailed account of Sundar's stay.

His needs were very simple. Dewan Appasamy, anxious to be a good host, tried to discover what Sundar liked best in the way of food and drink, but beyond saying he liked any beverage to be very hot, Sundar was not forthcoming on the subject, and quite happily ate whatever he was given. He spent his days at Shenbaganur in walking, meditating and working away at his English. His visit to South India had involved the use of interpreters to translate Sundar's Hindustani into the local dialects. It became increasingly apparent that a fluency in English would be a considerable asset, enabling him to preach throughout India without constant recourse to an interpreter. In the event, Sundar's decision to acquire a fluency in English was amply justified for within two years, Sundar was to be called upon to preach in England and America.

His weeks at Shenbaganur were primarily a holiday and Sundar gladly refreshed his spirit walking through the beautiful countryside, delighting in what he called the 'book of Nature'. The natural world was precious as a revelation of God at work. Time and again he was to draw upon the workings of nature to illustrate a point.

The Church needs to be flooded by the power of the Holy Spirit in the way the Indian plains are inundated by the fresh streams flowing from the Himalayas; frequent communion with God is as necessary to the Christian as rising to the surface of the water for air is to some fish. We have already seen the use Sundar made of these two parables. There were many more from the natural world. Trying to be like Our Lord will protect us from evil, as the camouflage of animals protects them from predators. This last comparison was elaborated by Sundar in his book *Reality and Religion* (Macmillan, 1924) in the chapter 'Christ Our Refuge'. He wrote, "To be safe from all attacks and dangers from the enemy, we must, by living in fellowship with the Lord, become like him. In snowy countries, Nature clothes animals and birds in white so that they are of one colour with surrounding environment and are thus secure from attacks."

No doubt the flora and fauna at Shenbaganur furnished him with many more parables of nature. Sundar also valued the conversations he had with his host. Dewan Appasamy had retired from his lawyer's practice in his mid-fifties and had devoted the last seventeen years to a life of prayer, study and evangelism. Sundar and he had much in common both in background and outlook.

Sundar had originally been invited to stay at Shenbaganur for two months, but after six weeks he began to feel restless. Refreshed by his leisure in the home of an understanding host, he left in May for Ceylon. A Methodist businessman, K. R. Wilson, arranged for Sundar to spend some days in Colombo and organised public meetings in the Town Hall. At one such, Sundar was approached by a woman who asked him to visit her twelve-year-old son in hospital. The boy had had an operation for an acute internal disorder. In the opinion of the hospital it would be months before the boy was on his feet. Indeed his eventual recovery was by no means assured. Perhaps remembering the sick people of Trivandram who had persistently followed him in search of healing, Sundar refused the woman's request. Maybe her crestfallen face haunted his thoughts for, on the next day, he went to the hospital to see her son.

Sundar asked the lad what he wanted him to do.

"Would you pray for me and lay your hand on my head?" said the young boy eagerly.

"I am not God, you know," Sundar replied gently. "I myself cannot heal you but Jesus can if you believe."

"I do understand that, but it would be a great comfort to hear you pray for me."

Up to this point their conversation had been conducted through interpreters. Sundar guessed that the boy might prefer the prayer to be in English, but Sundar was not yet fluent in the language and he asked if he would mind if the prayer was in Hindustani.

"I shall not mind what language you use, Sadhu."

Sundar placed his hands on the boy's head and prayed aloud. Then he bade the young patient good-bye and left the ward. The boy's condition rapidly deteriorated. His temperature rose at an alarming rate. The hospital summoned his parents, fearing that he was at the point of death. His mother and father sat anxiously by his bedside until his temperature began to drop. Within a short while it returned to normal. Two days later the boy was well enough to leave hospital. He had made a dramatic recovery. In a week he was well enough to attend a meeting addressed by Sundar and greeted him afterwards.

Sundar was not surprised that the boy was healed. He believed in miracles, and had himself been saved from death by what he believed to be divine intervention. Why should one question or be amazed at the power of God? This capacity to accept miracles was one he felt the world was losing. In a reference to the materialism rife in the world, which in Europe and America was to shock him even more than it did in India, he later said, "The days of miracles are not over, but the days of faith are past."

The healing of that young patient in the Colombo hospital testified to the power of Jesus Christ and to its availability through prayer and faith. This was Sundar's view and he did not wonder at God's healing grace. He did wonder however at people's obstinacy in failing to realise that it was God who healed and not Sundar Singh. Sundar tried so hard to get this point across. As news of the boy's recovery spread it became necessary to convince people that he was not a miracle worker. Sundar wrestled with this problem. Jesus had healed the sick and had commissioned the apostles to do likewise.

> "Faith will bring with it these miracles: believers will cast out devils in my name and speak in strange tongues; if they handle snakes or drink any deadly poison, they will come to no harm; and the sick on whom they lay their hands will recover."
>
> So after talking with them the Lord Jesus was taken up into heaven, and he took his seat at the right hand of God; but they went out to make their proclamation everywhere, and the Lord worked with them and confirmed their words by the miracles that followed. (St Mark 16 : 17–20 NEB).

If this healing power had been transmitted to his hands could he set it aside? Sundar had to decide and eventually made his decision. He would not lay hands on a sick person again or pray in public for a specific healing. Among his friends there were those who regretted this policy but Sundar stood firm. He would not risk anything that might appear possibly to detract from the absolute primacy of Jesus. He would not risk anything that might cause unthinking people to impute to him that which belonged to Christ and to Christ alone. His determination was strengthened by the thought of his unworthiness. Had he not torn up and burned a Bible with his own two hands? The memory of that childish outburst in adolescence was never to leave him. He seemed to feel that his hands were permanently stained and he refrained even from extending them in blessing.

Professor Friedrich Heiler, the German theologian, whose admiration for Sundar Singh was first aroused when he was asked to review Streeter and Appasamy's *The Sadhu* wrote his own study of Sundar in 1924. Called *Sadhu Sundar Singh, Ein Apostel des Ostens und Westens* it was translated into English by Olive Wyon under the title *The Gospel of Sadhu Sundar*

Singh (George Allen & Unwin 1927). Professor Heiler believed that it was in this year 1918, when Sundar was in South India, that he had an experience which was parallel to Christ's temptation in the wildnerness. In his own book *At the Master's Feet* (Madras 1923) Sundar writes of the event without giving a precise date. It seems likely as Professor Heiler suggests that it did occur at this period. We need to remember that Sundar had in a short time become an illustrious public preacher to whom thousands flocked to listen. He had to adjust to this new status, to prevent himself being knocked off course by it. This temptation experience may well have been part of the 'adjusting' process.

Sundar decribed how he had gone outside alone to pray. While in prayer he had been approached by a man whose manner though dignified roused in Sundar a measure of suspicion and hostility. This visitor no doubt lived only in Sundar's mind but was none the less menacing for that. He begged Sundar's pardon for disturbing him and explained that he felt his intrusion was justified as he only sought the welfare of other people.

This was his plea, that Sundar should become a great religious leader, not merely in respect of Christians but also of the millions of Hindus and Moslems in India. There would be far more reward for Sundar if he complied with this suggestion than he had ever received through his Christian ministry. Sundar would gain the ultimate reward, the worship of his followers. Sundar recognised his adversary.

"My reward is my Lord. Get thee hence, Satan!" he replied. The powerful evil that had threatened him drove Sundar to tears of exhaustion as he prayed for strength. As the evil departed he was aware of the presence of Jesus and gradually his peace of mind returned.

Professor Heiler commented:

Thus Sundar Singh overcame one of the greatest temptations of his life, the temptation to tamper with his vocation. In its essence the temptation consisted of this; why should he not become a great Indian guru . . .; and why should not Christianity be included in a system which would give Jesus, like Mohammed and Buddha, a place among the chief *avatara* of the great Saviour-Deity?

We may wonder why Sundar who had already endured so much for his Christian faith, and whose devotion to his Saviour had been sorely tried and tested, should be subject to a temptation so naïve. Since we know that he put this siren voice far from him, we tend perhaps to underrate the pressures to which he was being subjected at this time. We should remember that Sundar was an Indian proud of his country, living at a time when a nationalist movement was gathering momentum. This was the India of Gandhi, an India that questioned British rule and was reaching out towards independence. Sundar had often lamented the Anglo-European cultural strait-jacket of the Church in India. The feasibility of leading an inter-faith alliance embracing all shades of India's spiritual inheritance, might momentarily have had its appeal. To so gifted a leader the proposition had its challenge and allure. Yet Sundar cared little for political considerations and such an idea when more closely examined would obviously seem a foolish dream.

After his tour of Ceylon, Sundar returned to South India and in July was able to renew and deepen his friendship with the Parkers. With Rebecca Parker in particular Sundar felt an immediate rapport. From this time on they were to correspond regularly. Rebecca Parker suggested she might write a book about Sundar's ministry. She intended originally to write a short account in the local language for the people of Travancore, but when this had been completed she set to work on the fuller English biography referred to earlier in this chapter. This was finished in September 1918 and published by the Christian Literature Society for India.

Sundar was again caught up in a succession of public meetings, which exhausted him mentally and physically. An attack of influenza was followed by a brief recuperation as the guest of the poet Rabindranath Tagore. Fortunately a leisurely autumn sea voyage en route to Burma gave him a chance to rest.

From Burma he sailed for Singapore and Malaya. It was at Singapore that Sundar first preached in English. Through a misunderstanding no interpreter was available. The moment he had viewed so apprehensively had come. Sundar had to take the plunge. Although he felt his English was inadequate, the circumstances gave him little choice. A month or two later he remarked to a reporter from *The Christian Patriot*, "When I preach in English I feel an 'earthquake' in me. As when fire and other matters under the earth cannot escape there is an earthquake, so, when thoughts in my heart have no means of escape, my heart quakes."

A letter in *The Christian Patriot* from Sundar himself announced that he planned to follow his visit to Singapore and Malaya with a tour of Japan and China. He hoped to go on from China directly to Tibet, and in his letter he again invited anyone who wished to meet the Maharishi of Kailash to accompany him. Sundar had now been travelling through India and beyond its shores since the autumn of 1917. It was now 1919 and Tibet called to him and began to fill his thoughts.

Perhaps because he was wearied by such a prolonged absence from home Sundar was also a little disillusioned about some of the foreign countries he'd visited. Some stringent criticisms were to be found in certain of his comments, notably about Japan which, he informed a friend, had "plunged herself in the soul-killing floods of Western materialism". He was shocked to discover that Buddhist temples were thronged not with worshippers but with tourists, and he gained the impression that religion now played a minor role in the lives of the Japanese people.

His plans to go to Tibet straight from China were thwarted as fighting had broken out on the China–Tibet border. He was obliged to return by boat back to India and would then proceed to Tibet along his usual route. On arrival in Madras he attended a meeting and ended his address with these words, "I am going to the hills and to Tibet; it is quite uncertain whether I shall be able to return, so serious are some of the risks attending the journey and my work in the regions beyond. Even if I do not see you again in this world I hope to meet you in heaven amidst the new life and its surroundings. I wish you good-bye until we meet again."

There were serious risks but risks he yearned to take. Soon Sundar was hastening north towards the Himalayas. Summer had come, and with it the melting of the snows which made entry into Tibet possible. Sundar did not wish to waste a single day.

9

A NUMBER OF people had responded to Sundar's invitation to accompany him on another expedition to visit the Maharishi of Kailash. While Sundar had been travelling he had been difficult to contact. In his absence however, plans for the venture had been laid and the expenses underwritten by K. R. Wilson, who had organised Sundar's visit to Ceylon the previous summer. Mr Wilson was himself intending to join the party. It was arranged that the expedition should leave from Almora, a village some fifty miles from the Tibetan border. By coincidence this departure point had also been chosen by another group, three European women who were also preparing for Sundar to guide them to the Maharishi.

These women with a party of twenty-one coolies and a mountain of provisions had already left Almora two days before Sundar's boat docked in Bombay. One of the Europeans, Mary Dobson, daughter of the English poet Austin Dobson, was particularly eager to meet the Maharishi, and had written several letters to Sundar on the subject during his travels abroad. She was already acquainted with Sundar. Since their first meeting in 1917 his personality and his teaching had greatly impressed her. In his accounts of his visits to the Maharishi, Sundar referred to an early Greek manuscript of the New Testament from which the Maharishi had read. Mary Dobson with an interest in Biblical scholarship was keen to see the manuscript.

Unfortunately the letters she had sent to Sundar never reached him, consequently he had no knowledge of her plans. Mary and her companions, after covering the distance between Almora and Badrinath, remained at Badrinath a week hoping that Sundar would join them. When he did not arrive they regretfully turned back. It is unlikely they would have been able to cross into Tibet in any event since at that time Europeans were being refused entry. Mary Dobson found a letter from Sundar which had been forwarded to her at a post a few miles along their return journey. From this it was apparent that Sundar had not received any of her letters outlining the plans for the journey.

Meanwhile the preparations of the other group were also proving to be abortive for a similar reason—lack of communication with Sundar. Journeying northwards Sundar made for Kotgarh quite unaware that his presence was required at Almora. He only learned this when he had already reached Kotgarh, but by this time he was suffering from an injury to his foot. The wound stubbornly refused to heal. It became obvious that if the party at Almora were going to wait for him first to recover and then to make the awkward two-hundred-mile journey from Kotgarh, that they would be delayed by many weeks. Sundar suggested that they made their own way towards Kailash and that he would meet them en route. He could enter Tibet at a point farther north and save himself the journey to Almora.

However, the party at Almora decided that it was too risky to make the journey without Sundar to guide them, and reluctantly the project was abandoned.

This was the last attempt Sundar ever made to get witnesses who would prove that the Maharishi existed, and he himself never revisited the hermit. By the time his foot healed it was too late to go so far into Tibet that summer. Why he did not visit the Maharishi on any later occasion is unclear. It is possible that he felt that the speculation aroused by the mere mention of the Maharishi hindered rather than helped the task of Christian evangelism which was the primary aim of his life.

All the attempts to conduct others to the Maharishi had proved unsuccessful which only went to prove that the sort of Tibetan journey Sundar undertook so lightly, meant for other people months of detailed planning, mounds of luggage and considerable financial backing.

The failure of the two expeditions to Kailash did not rule out the chance of a more modest preaching tour in Tibet and in July Sundar left Kotgarh with Thaniyat, a Tibetan friend.

Their main enemy was the intense cold. Their route through Yangpa took them higher and higher into the mountains. By the time they reached the Hangpu La Pass they were at a height of 19,000 feet. Although discouraged by the sight of three bodies frozen to death, they nonetheless pressed on to the next village.

This summer they seemed to be more warmly received than on earlier visits. Even the lamas were prepared to give them a hearing and offered them hospitality on occasion. In one village the lamas suggested they cut Sundar's hair for him, a proposal he welcomed. He was somewhat surprised when they returned to do the job with a pair of sheep-shearing scissors!

Again Sundar found the dirtiness of the unwashed Tibetan villagers almost beyond belief. They for their part were similarly astonished at his cleanliness. On one occasion he noticed a boy look first at his own filthy hands and then at Sundar's clean ones. Without a word the lad went to the stream and began scrubbing the dirt off. He returned with pride to compare them again. Sundar later used this incident in one of his books to illustrate how people are often influenced more by what one is than by what one says.

Before recrossing into India Sundar and Thaniyat visited a company of Tibetan Christians at Tsering just inside the border. They were delighted to find this small Christian community in good heart. One young boy wanted to return to India with Sundar but his mother forbade him. Sundar hoped that when the boy was older his parents would allow him to join Sundar in India for training as an evangelist.

Back in north India after his Tibetan journey Sundar had two important visits to make. The first was to Dr Wherry, his former headmaster at the Ludhiana school, and the second to his father at Rampur. Sundar was sure of a welcome from Dr Wherry who had watched his progress over the years with a close and affectionate interest.

Less certain was he of the reception he would get at his father's home. Ever since he had left his family home, Sundar had hoped and prayed that his father might relent in his attitude, make his peace with his son, and that he might come to accept for himself the Christian faith. Now, fourteen years after his expulsion from home his longfelt hope was realised. When Sundar arrived his father welcomed him warmly and shared with his son the glad news that he, like Sundar, now believed the Christian Gospel. Sundar was profoundly moved by his father's words.

"You must baptise me, son," Sher Singh said later that first day.

"Listen, father. I cannot baptise you. You must go to one of the churches and ask the minister to baptise you. I cannot change my rule even for you. Many people have asked me to baptise them and I have always refused because I believe it is the Church's task not mine."

Sher Singh regretfully agreed and as it happened he was never baptised. Sher Singh was to live for almost another four years and it remains a mystery why he never chose to present himself for baptism during this time.

Father and son had much to talk over during the few days Sundar spent in Rampur. Sundar explained how invitations were pouring in from every corner of the world for him to come and preach.

"You must accept as many as you can," said Sher Singh. "I will pay your fares."

Thus it was that on 16th January 1920 Sundar was aboard the *City of Cairo* in a second-class berth as the ship left Bombay for Liverpool. A voyage of twenty-five days lay before him giving ample time for him to prepare himself for the meetings, services and receptions which lay ahead in Britain.

Why did he choose England? Two reasons. First, Sundar wished to decide for himself whether it was true, as so many people in India had told him, that European Christianity was on the way out, that its influence was on the wane in the manners and morals of the European nations. Secondly, and more importantly, Sundar felt convinced that God was calling him to visit England.

Sundar was met at Liverpool by a friend Willie Hindle. His first night in England was spent at the home of Willie Hindle's sister, the mother of five-year-old twins. Willie left Sundar with the twins for a few minutes and was amused to find the three of them romping on the floor when he returned. The children's friendly informality helped to rid Sundar of his initial nervousness in a strange country. Willie's sister later told him of the conversation she had with the twins at breakfast the next day after Willie and Sundar had left the house.

"Mummy," said one little boy, "where has Jesus gone to?"

"That wasn't Jesus," said his mother, "that was Sadhu Sundar Singh."

"No, Mummy," insisted her son, "I know who he was. That was Jesus. And I know where he's gone to. He's gone to heaven and taken Uncle Willie with him."

Sundar's second host in England was Dr Rendel Harris,

Mary Dobson's cousin. From Dr Harris's Manchester home Sundar went to Birmingham, to Kingsmead, a Quaker missionary college, where he stayed with the Warden, J. W. Hoyland and his wife. Their letters to their son who was working in India reveal the pleasure they received from Sundar's visit from the moment when Mr Hoyland first greeted him at the station. Against the drab greyness of a railway platform, Sundar appeared a colourful figure in his saffron robe. The Hoylands were sympathetic hosts and tried to ensure that Sundar had plenty of time on his own and a chance to adjust to the faster pace of Western life. Mrs Hoyland wrote to her son, "It's wonderful having Sundar Singh here; it's unlike anything else that has ever happened; it is indescribable but it is like having Christ in the house as near as one could imagine what that would be like."

From Manchester Sundar travelled south to Oxford, where his arrival was eagerly awaited by Aiyadurai Appasamy (later Bishop Appasamy) who at that time was engaged in postgraduate studies. He had not yet met Sundar but had of course heard a great deal about him particularly from his father.

Sundar's meetings with undergraduates and university dons were well attended and everywhere people fell under his spell. Many felt, as Mrs Hoyland had, that they were in the presence of Christ. Sometimes in their enthusiasm they misinterpreted his words. One young man reading theology decided to dispense with further training and told his principal that he desired to start work as a missionary at once. Sundar had to explain that this was not what he had meant. The student should continue with necessary studies but also remember that academic training alone would not suffice.

Sundar's English hosts were eager to know what impressions he was forming of England and of the state of Church life in this country. It was not long before someone asked him the question outright. Sundar hesitated, torn between courtesy and truthfulness.

"I have not been in England very long, so what I say at this moment is not a considered opinion. I do feel however that religion in England does not give much peace. The things of the spirit can only be known with quiet and meditation. People here rush about so that they do not have time for prayer."

When asked weeks later why he had come to England he confirmed that first impression.

"Some Indians believe," he smiled, "that there is no real religion in England but you send missionaries to India as a matter of policy. I wanted to see for myself. I have found that you are a very busy people, and that you have so much to do that there does not seem much time to think about religion. There is a great deal of materialism. But when I get into your homes and know you then it is I find you really do care about religion." Sundar was to spend a further six months in the industrialised societies of England, America and Australia. By the end of that time his criticisms were to become more caustic as he became increasingly disenchanted with the West's pre-occupation with materialistic values.

Sundar was sternly critical of the bustle and urgency of modern life. He felt all this 'busyness' was inimical to the life of the Spirit in man. Now, fifty years later, we can see even more clearly the accuracy of his assessment.

Yet, true though that assessment was, we may wonder whether Sundar was sufficiently well-informed about the situation in Britain to interpret the signs correctly. Certainly he saw about him evidence of the decline in the privileged position and status of institutional religion, a decline which had been greatly accelerated by the traumatic experience of the 1914–18 war. Did he see, could he be expected to see, that the indications of numerical decline were also tokens of a new challenge to the Church? In losing prestige, the Church had become less hypocritical. The doubts and self-criticism indicated not only a shaken confidence but a desire for fresh honesty and realism. It was a situation in which there were seeds of hope. It is not possible to tell how far Sundar was aware of these positive factors. It was partly on account of this very search for new insights and illumination that Sundar's message with its clarity and simplicity was so well received.

March 1920 saw him in London speaking to an audience in Church House, Westminster, which represented all shades of churchmanship in the church of England. It was a full house and hundreds were turned away. A *Church Times* correspondent commented, "Did the clergy, I wondered, see in those thronging thousands a rebuke to their own too frequent failure to preach the Gospel of Jesus Christ in its attractive simplicity? Perhaps they tell themselves it is the strange novelty of the preacher that draws. But they won't believe it—at least not quite."

Sundar himself had to adjust to the unfamiliar novelties of English life. The demands of a preaching tour were strenuous enough in his homeland. In England Sundar had the added strain of new faces, unusual food, and unpredictable weather. That he could take all this in his stride testifies to his resilience and to the inward peace that sustained him.

The London fog was quite a shock! Sundar had a favourite anecdote about it. He and two friends had paused on the edge of the pavement unable to see a foot in front of them. The dense mist distorted both distance and colour. Sundar's long robe stood out more than most of the surroundings in the fog, to the confusion of a woman who mistook him for a pillar box. Her startled expression when the letter box said, "Give me the letter. I'll post it!" appealed to Sundar's sense of humour.

Meanwhile, A. J. Appasamy and his tutor, Canon B. H.

Streeter, suggested that they should collect material for a book on Sundar's teaching. Sundar gave his permission so Appasamy travelled with him taking notes of his public addresses and also sitting in on discussions with smaller groups. He arranged for Sundar to meet the distinguished Roman Catholic lay theologian Baron von Hugel. Von Hugel had read Rebecca Parker's book and was keen to discuss personally with Sundar questions the book had raised in his own mind.

It seemed to Von Hugel that Sundar set too little store by membership of the Church. His thoughts on the matter were set out in a memorandum he sent to A. J. Appasamy a fortnight after the interview which the latter summarised in his book *Sundar Singh.*

> While the Baron was fully aware of the value of the Sadhu's characteristic contribution to Indian Christianity, he was troubled by his individualism and pleaded in the memorandum that he should attach himself far more closely to the Christian Church . . . The Baron felt that the humility of Sundar Singh was not complete until he was willing to accept the authority of the Church more fully than he did.

The tentative manner in which Baron von Hugel worded this criticism indicates that for the most part he was impressed by Sundar Singh and the rest of the memorandum confirms this.

Sundar's ecumenical attitude gave rise to constant controversy. It is remarkable that at a time when denominational barriers were generally unyielding that so many of his contemporaries conceded that Sundar was a special case. The Archbishop of Canterbury, Dr Randall Davidson, who received Sundar at Lambeth Palace said, in connection with Sundar's quite indiscriminate acceptance of invitations from all denominations, "That is quite all right—for *you.*"

Professor Friedrich Heiler wrote to Sundar a few years later to inquire about his interview with Von Hugel. Heiler was gathering material for a second book about Sundar Singh, *Apostel Oder Betruger?* (Apostle or Impostor?), an answer to the attacks on Sundar's integrity which were growing apace at that time. Sundar's written reply helps us to clarify his position vis-à-vis the institutional Church.

> Concerning my membership in the Church, I must say that I belong to the Body of Christ, that means, to the true Church which cannot be understood as a building of tiles and stones but as a body of true Christians, living and dead, visible and invisible. But I have nothing against anyone becoming a member of an organised Church on earth. In this sense I am a member of the Church of England in India . . . I also believe in the Eucharist and in Baptism. Every Christian indeed has to obey the commands of the Lord concerning these Sacraments, because they are the means of great blessing; not because the Eucharist becomes the true body of Christ or because there is anything special in Water, Bread or Wine but because of the obedience towards our Lord. Of course, all this depends on faith. With the exception of the Roman Church, I receive the Lord's Supper, the Holy Communion, in every Church.

A short holiday in Paris with his friend A. J. Appasamy, further meetings in England, a visit to Ireland and another to Scotland. There was no time to spare, no chance of accepting the three hundred invitations still outstanding. Sundar was due in the United States by 30th May.

On arrival his colourful appearance, his oriental background, his refusal to make money out of his tour, even his lack of luggage made him immediately newsworthy. To most

American churchmen he was an unknown quantity. Accustomed to a succession of pundits coming from India to market their own brand of Eastern mysticism, there were those who wondered if Sundar was such another. As they soon discovered, he was not. His Gospel was the Christ of Galilee. He did not proclaim an Indian Christianity, nor indeed English or American versions. The Christianity of the New Testament was what he gave them, delivered in a compelling manner that opened their eyes anew.

Sundar's visit coincided with a student conference held during June at Silver Bay on the shores of Lake George in New York State. He was asked to attend. In this romantic lakeside setting Sundar spoke at an open-air rally one evening. He stood with his back to the lake. The setting sun outlined the mountain horizon. The scene was reminiscent of the Sea of Galilee two thousand years earlier. His words to the student audience at Silver Bay were, in effect, addressed to America as a whole. America, said Sundar, was near the Kingdom but not of it, and illustrated this in a parable. A hunter was being chased by a tiger, but he was not afraid because he knew he was nearing a shelter and had the key to it. At least he thought he had, but when he reached the shelter he discovered the key was not after all in his possession. Only the thickness of the door stood between him and safety yet he was doomed. Many Americans were, he thought, like the hunter. They knew wherein their salvation lay but did not make use of it.

Although he had now been away from India for seven months, Sundar still had one further tour before his return. From San Francisco he travelled to Australia where he stayed for a month. His programme followed the usual pattern of crowded meetings attended by Christians of all denominations.

While in Adelaide he celebrated his thirty-first birthday. He was at the peak of his influence, in every way a commanding figure. The ill health that was to dog him in his later thirties and prematurely age him had not yet shown itself. The Revd. J. H. Deane, Principal of the New Zealand Bible Training Institute of Auckland, wrote thirty years later to Bishop Appasamy giving his impressions of Sundar at that time. "I was then in my final year at the Sydney University and met and conducted the Sadhu round the University, introduced him to the Christian group that had then been formed, and had him speak to the students who cared to assemble and hear him. He was a unique figure, dressed in his saffron robe and wearing sandals, with an unwrinkled, radiant face, full bearded, with a certain calm and majesty of countenance. He seemed to me, as a young Christian, the nearest that I could imagine our Lord looked like. He spoke quietly but with obvious spiritual power; and he spoke simply, with constant reference to the common things to be found in nature to illustrate the profoundest spiritual truths."

His Australian tour completed, Sundar was now ready to return to India. He had arranged for Vincent David to meet him and keep his arrival secret. Sundar had seen enough of crowds and receptions for a while. In the company of Vincent he was glad to relax after nine strenuous months of constant travelling. He gave Vincent his impressions of the West. He spoke of the materialism and the hectic pace of life which threatened to crowd out religion. Yet he had met many whose Christian faith was deep-rooted and genuine. He concluded that there are no Christian countries only individual Christians within those countries.

10

SABATHU WITH ITS quiet village life and breathtaking beauty provided the rest Sundar needed. The previous nine months had taken their toll of him in body and mind. The strain of such a programme had exacted more from him physically than was first realised. He had sacrificed himself in many ways. He had been denied adequate time for prayer. He had had to forsake a summer tour of Tibet in 1920, a matter for real regret. Yet he was sure his decision to visit England, America and Australia had been the right one. He had felt it to be God's will for him. Sundar had however underestimated the demands these tours would make on him, and had not foreseen how oppressive to his soul the bustling materialism of the West would prove to be.

The winter of 1920–21 at Sabathu renewed him and as the first buds of spring appeared he eagerly turned his mind once more in the direction of Tibet.

In May 1921 he set out from Sabathu and was later joined at Kotgarh by a European companion named Wright. As so often happened conditions that Sundar took in his stride proved too much for his friend. The weather on the Rotang Pass was particularly bitter, causing peeling of the skin. The combination of intense cold and high altitude forced them to return. Wright's health was not able to withstand exposure to such severe weather.

Sundar, having assured himself that Mr Wright would be cared for at Simla, was keen to return to Tibet. His second excursion was in the company of a young Tibetan for whom the climate presented no problems.

On his last tour of Tibet in 1919 his reception in the villages had been more welcoming and though this more favourable pattern continued the trip was not to be without incident.

Sundar was walking some way ahead of his companion in desolate terrain when he heard and saw a wild yak careering straight for him. Sundar made for the only escape the region offered, a high rock. He scrambled to the top. The yak circled the rock snorting with frustration. There did not seem much that Sundar could do except hope the yak would soon lose interest! He settled down to wait. Fortunately his friend was not far behind and had meanwhile met up with some other travellers. Seeing Sundar's situation, they rushed forward, shouting and throwing stones at the yak until it made off. They were just celebrating Sundar's escape when they encountered another hazard of Tibetan travel. During the commotion bandits had crept up and surrounded them. They took all the travellers' luggage and the little group feared for their lives. It was Sundar who saved the day. He began talking to their assailants. Reluctant and impatient at first, they eventually agreed to give the holy man a hearing perhaps feeling a superstitious respect for his sadhu's robes. Sundar's gentle but firm authority and obvious goodness came across to them. The bandits despite their alarming appearance and fearsome reputation were basically simple men, and soon fell under Sundar's influence. They cheerfully gave the travellers back their goods and prepared to set the seal on their change of heart by making each of their visitors a cup of Tibetan tea flavoured with salt and butter. Sundar looked at his cup doubtfully.

"If you don't mind,' he said cautiously, "I would like first to wash this cup."

"Certainly," said one of their hosts, "but we cannot allow you, our guest, to clean it." He took the cup from Sundar, stuck out his very long tongue and licked it clean.

"There," he said proudly and poured in the tea. Sundar

could not bring himself to drink it. He used the tea to wash out the cup. The bandits watched with amazement. Fortunately for everyone they seemed to find it all hilariously funny.

"You must understand," said one of the travellers trying to explain Sundar's behaviour, "Indians always wash dishes before they use them."

At this the bandits fell into further paroxysms of laughter.

"There's no point in that," giggled one of them. "If it's necessary to wash the dishes, you ought also to wash out your stomach every day."

Eventually their mirth subsided. Sundar thanked them for their hospitality. It was getting late and time to leave.

"No, you mustn't go now. It is getting dark and would be dangerous to travel now. You are our friends. Sleep here in the cave. You will be safe with us." Thankfully they accepted this offer and slept there until morning.

We are not told any further details of this Tibetan mission but their return was hastened by early falls of snow which threatened to block the passes, and in September they crossed the border back into India.

To Sundar it was a homecoming to a stack of letters and invitations all waiting his attention. Many European countries had been disappointed that he had not been able to visit them the previous year. From Switzerland, Germany, Holland and the Scandinavian countries came pressing requests. Sundar came to the conclusion that he should accept wherever possible so plans were laid for another European tour during 1922. One invitation gave him special pleasure. Sir William Willcocks, Chief Engineer and Architect of the Aswan Dam had read the book *The Sadhu* by Streeter and Appasamy. He was deeply moved by what he read and eager to meet Sundar personally. He suggested that Sundar might like to spend a holiday with him in Palestine en route for his European tour.

As we have seen Sundar strove in many ways to copy Our Lord's way of life. His life as a sadhu, his fast, his method of preaching all followed the blueprint of Jesus's life. A pilgrimage to the Holy Land had long been Sundar's ambition, and he gladly accepted.

In January 1922 Sundar left for the Holy Land. Jerusalem was their base. Each day Sir William drove his guest to the holy places associated with Our Lord's life. Under pressure from the Bishop of Jerusalem Sundar agreed to preach in St George's Cathedral, but he stressed that he had come to the Holy Land to learn rather than teach. Sundar traced Our Lord's steps in the Garden of Gethsemane, along the Way of the Cross and in all the sites hallowed by Christ's Passion.

Meanwhile in Switzerland preparations were underway for his imminent tour. Sundar arrived in Lausanne on 27th February. That evening the committee who had arranged the tour outlined their plans. Sundar was quite happy to leave the arrangements to them but he made one proviso. He would only speak once each day. He knew he could not give of his best if the programme was too crowded. On one occasion in Zürich, Miss Goodwin the secretary who accompanied him to all his meetings in Switzerland, noted in her diary the effect of his being persuaded to address two meetings in quick succession. She wrote, "He was not at his best, because he had not time for quiet prayer and preparation." Her diary reveals glimpses of a man who was often tired and growing increasingly impatient, even testy, with the publicity and attention he received at every turn. She writes for example of his neglect of a bunch of red and white carnations given him at a railway station. He thanked the donor, placed them on the carriage seat beside him where they would have remained had not Miss Goodwin rescued them. She recalls him wiping a steamy train window with a letter from an admirer.

This impatience began to show through in his public addresses. He became more and more forthright in his comments on European Christianity, almost as if he found it hard to believe that the churches in Europe could be so blind to the shortcomings that he saw so clearly.

The burden of his message was simple. The malady of the churches of the West was their prayerlessness. At one meeting attended by pastors of the Swiss churches, one pastor asked Sundar for advice on how they might make their work more effective. This was his answer, "Be men of prayer, and everything else, inner peace, a knowledge of daily duties, sacrificing love, service to one's neighbour, these will all come by themselves. Put aside every morning some time for quiet meditation on the Word of God and for prayer and your life will be wonderfully changed. Without daily intercourse with God there is no piety, no Christianity, no real life."

The harsher note that now characterised his preaching was not welcomed in every quarter. Some of his listeners were annoyed at what seemed to them effrontery. What did this young Indian know of church life in Europe? What business had he to condemn?

At Leipzig in Germany the editor of a church paper took issue with him on his teaching on prayer. Sundar had said that prayer was not a matter of begging but primarily of union with God. The editor wrote that Sundar's preaching on prayer was in conflict with that of Christ, and went on to list what he felt to be further inconsistencies in Sundar Singh's message. He ended his article by saying, "We decline in any way to judge the Sadhu as a person. If anyone says that he has fellowship with God, or that he is a disciple of Jesus as few are, we do not dare contradict him. We do doubt however whether he justifies the title 'Apostle of India' or whether he proclaims fully the old gospel."

Sundar's health was not as robust as it was formerly. The rigours of his expeditions to Tibet would by themselves have taxed his health. To these were now added the very different but nonetheless exacting pressures of tours to the British Isles, Europe, America and Australia. Gone was the time when a week or two's rest would restore him to peak fitness. Indifferent health may well have partially accounted for his somewhat pessimistic estimate of European Christianity on this tour. There were times when he seemed to despair of his ability to penetrate the European mind.

While travelling in Sweden Sundar visited the tomb of Swedenborg at Uppsala. Emanuel Swedenborg, an eighteenth-century Swedish scientist and mystic, had devoted much of his life to showing, by purely scientific analysis, the spiritual structure of the Universe. In the course of his studies he became aware of the presence of the supernatural world, partly through his dreams but also when awake. His beliefs are still propagated by Swedenborg churches in Europe, America and Australia. Sundar knew enough about Swedenborg to know that the latter had, like himself, had many visionary experiences. Sundar regretted that he had not read Swedenborg's writings, and he promised himself he would remedy this on his return to India.

After Sweden, Norway and Denmark, one more country remained to be visited. Sundar arrived in Holland in May. A Dutch translation of Rebecca Parker's book had appeared two years before and his name was already widely known. At Rotterdam, during the final month of his tour, Sundar was sternly critical of Western Christianity which he felt had lost its way. Europe which owed so much to Christianity in its culture, its freedom and its education, was in danger of denying Christ. "Europe is like Judas Iscariot," claimed Sundar. "It eats with Christ and then denies him."

When Sundar first set foot in England on the earlier European tour he had hoped to discover at first hand the true facts about the state of the Church in Europe. He had first heard the Gospel from Europeans and Americans and had supposed that these men in their devoted service reflected a strong and faithful church in their own country. When he heard it said that the missionaries might be better employed evangelising the country from whence they came he could not believe it.

He now however had many months' knowledge of the Church in the West and his words to the people of Rotterdam, his accusation that Europe had betrayed her Lord, were the words of a disappointed man. Appraised of the true facts he all the more appreciated the steadfastness and loyalty of countless individuals whose deep thirst for God testified to the work of the Holy Spirit. With this thought to encourage him he bade farewell to the people of Holland and returned thankfully to India, and to the peace of Sabathu once more.

From that time onwards, save for short expeditions into Tibet, Sundar was not to leave the shores of India. Another phase in his life had come to an end. When he was asked to make a second visit to America he refused saying that he intended to devote the remainder of his life to preaching in India and Tibet. He was unmoved by their flattering argument that he belonged not only to India but to the whole world. He returned to preaching in the villages of North India and addressing local conventions.

Another means of communication, the written word, offered him a chance to continue his international contacts. Until this time, apart from *A Collection of Incidents* written in 1915 and his newspaper letters in *Nur Afshan* he had committed none of his teaching to paper.

He was beginning to feel his own lack of education. He had left school at fifteen, and the only formal education he had received after that was during his year at St John's College, Lahore. After his disappearance in 1929 his friends found an invoice amongst his papers at Sabathu dated September 1922. It was from a bookseller in Bombay and it listed ten books he had ordered. Their subjects ranged from anthropology to philosophy.

Sher Singh, Sundar's father, died in April 1923 leaving half his considerable estate to Sundar. He had already discussed the matter of his Will with his son and Sundar had failed to persuade his father that he, Sundar, did not need a financial legacy. Sher Singh wanted Sundar to buy himself a house where he could rest between his preaching tours. He was also eager to guarantee Sundar a secure old age, and in his Will left him land and money for this purpose. Sundar was quite certain he would never reach old age and gave the land to his brother. He did however buy himself a house, not the bungalow his father had envisaged, but a ramshackle old mission house in the poorest quarter of Sabathu.

Soon after he had moved in he invited A. J. Appasamy, who was now lecturing at Bishop's College, Calcutta, to visit him. In his biography of Sundar Singh, Appasamy records his first impressions of the house.

> I had to walk through the dirtiest and busiest part of the town to reach his house. His next-door neighbours belonged to the scavenger caste who often, in the quiet of the night, indulged in weird music or noisy quarrels. His house was on the edge of the town. From it I saw a magnificent view of the mountains. The house seemed to me a significant symbol of the two worlds with which Sundar Singh constantly tried to live in contact—the busy world of men, sometimes dirty and sordid, and the world of Nature so beautiful and calm.

The house was large, too large for one man's need, so Sundar gave over more than half the house to a friend, Dr Peoples. Dr Peoples was on the staff of the Sabathu Leper Hospital where Sundar and Samuel Stokes had worked temporarily in 1907. Dr Peoples took up residence in Sundar's house with his wife and four children. It was an ideal arrangement for Sundar still had the privacy of his own rooms but also had what he had missed ever since he left home, the background of a happy family life. He loved children and A. J. Appasamy soon noticed during his visit Sundar's happy way with Dr Peoples' children. With his health declining it was reassuring for his friends to know that if illness should overtake him he would be expertly cared for by Dr and Mrs Peoples.

A. J. Appasamy had been invited for the special purpose of assisting Sundar in the writing of a new book *Reality and Religion.* Although Sundar's spoken English was by now fluent he was not accustomed to writing in English. Thus it was that the manuscript of *Reality and Religion* was written originally in Urdu and with Appasamy's help translated into English.

Sundar's own preface explains his aim. He says, "In this little book I have put down some of the ideas and illustrations which are the outcome of my meditation. I am neither a philosopher nor a theologian, but a humble servant of the Lord, whose delight it is to meditate on the love of God and on the great wonders of His Creation." It was his consciousness of ultimate reality as it came to him in his prayer that he sought in this book to share with others.

As the year 1923 drew to a close Sundar's life had settled down to a quieter tempo. Yet still his purpose was the same as ever; to endeavour to convey to others the Glory that he had perceived.

11

Charles Andrews, Sundar's friend since 1907, had corresponded with Sundar during the years that followed but it was only rarely that they were able to meet. After a gap of several years they were able to spend some time together in 1926. In his memoir *Sadhu Sundar Singh* (Hodder and Stoughton 1934) Charles Andrews recalled his shock when he saw how Sundar had aged.

> . . . we met together at St Thomas's Church, Simla, when our mutual friend, Canon Chandu Lal, was also present with us. Sundar Singh had looked forward to this meeting and had come into Simla especially for that purpose . . . When the farewell moment came, a very strong impression was left upon my mind that we might never see each other again in this world.
>
> During that last meeting, as we conversed together, I noticed at once the marked physical change which had come over him. His face was strangely altered from the clear-cut features I had known of old. He had aged very rapidly indeed. Some internal disease seemed already to have obtained its fatal hold and undermined his constitution, making an obvious difference even in his outward appearance.

Charles Andrews was concerned about Sundar's health. Sundar had told him of his heart condition and although there were days when he felt no pain, there were other times when his discomfort was severe. There were other worries as well. In 1924 Sundar had had to turn back from a journey to Tibet, an occurrence which he described at the time in a letter to a friend, the Reverend H. A. Popley. ". . . I am sorry to say that owing to the weakness of my lungs I could not cross over high mountains on my way to Tibet and so I had to return. Hard work and continuous speaking for years in large meetings have affected my lungs, but I am feeling better now."

Before he met Charles Andrews in 1926 Sundar had had an operation on his left eye after eight months' discomfort and impaired sight. The operation was only partially successful and from then on he had to wear dark glasses to shield his eyes from the glare. It was only six years previously that a young student, J. H. Deane, had been so impressed with his fine physique and 'unwrinkled radiant face'. Things were now very different. Charles Andrews had sensed that for Sundar death was not far away. Sundar himself faced this probability for in May 1926 he confided to Thomas Riddle that although he had had three heart attacks the previous December, he still hoped to make one final foray into Tibet.

"I want once more to go to Tibet, and I will go via Almora. It has been revealed to me that my time is short now and I am very glad. I have only a great joy when I think of death."

His illness had slowed down the pace of his life but he had not been inactive. He was able to undertake short preaching tours and to address conventions. He also continued to write.

The purchase in 1923 of the house in Sabathu marked, as we see now with hindsight, the final phase of his life on earth. Sundar did most of his best writing in this period, and the years 1923–29 saw the publication of *Reality and Religion* (Macmillan & Co. 1924), *The Search After Reality* (Macmillan & Co. 1924), *Meditations on Various Aspects of the Spiritual Life* (Macmillan & Co. 1926), *Visions of the Spiritual World* (Macmillan & Co. 1926) and *With and Without Christ* (Cassell & Co. 1929).

In September 1924 he finished *The Search After Reality* in which he examined man's search for God as expressed within the Hindu, Buddhist, Moslem and Christian faiths.

Increasingly in his writing his attention was drawn towards life after death. Experiences of ecstasy in prayer, first in evidence after his sustained fast in 1913 had continued and become more frequent. During his last years these occurred as often as two or three times a month. When he was praying his spirit was able on occasions to 'walk in the glory of the heavenly sphere' to use Sundar's own description as found in the Preface to *Visions of the Spiritual World.* During the first of these visions the impressions had been so vivid that he thought he must have died. Their frequency and content were beyond his conscious control. As his own spirit wandered freely through what he called 'the world of the spirits' he was able to converse with the inhabitants. These conversations provided the material for *Visions of the Spiritual World* in which he gives a specific account of what happens to souls after death. In some detail he describes Heaven, Hell and the intermediate stages through which a soul progresses towards the 'fuller light of God'—a light not to be borne without preparation and instruction. The people Sundar met were not vague shadowy forms but individual and distinct personalities who were known by name but not the name by which they had been known on earth.

This is a perplexing book and presents problems for today's reader. It is explicit and highly coloured in its descriptions, it is sometimes harsh, sometimes complacent. Yet despite this, his view of the after-life as a journey of stages through which the soul progresses from darkness to light; the eternal possibility of those in Hell eventually entering Heaven; the implication that all may ultimately be saved—these are beliefs to which many Christians subscribe and to which Scripture testifies: "As in Adam all men die, so in Christ all will be brought to life." (1 Corinthians 15 : 22 NEB).

Dr H. B. Durrant, Bishop Lefroy's successor as Bishop of Lahore, was aware of the difficulties when he wrote the Foreword. He felt unqualified to answer questions on the exact nature of Sundar's visions, or the part played in them by the subconscious mind, or their objective reality. These questions were, in his view, irrelevant. "I felt," he wrote describing his reaction to reading the book, "that for me the veil which normally shrouds the real world, had been for a few moments lifted," and he compared Sundar's experience with that of Peter, James and John during Our Lord's Transfiguration.

In his book Sundar recounted what he had seen and heard in his visions. The degree to which these visions were coloured by personal factors, his particular character, his experience and his expectations, cannot be measured with a slide rule. That the visions were thus coloured is inevitable. In reading this book we need to remember that Sundar himself made it clear that for him the Bible came first and his ecstatic experiences second as revelations of the Divine Will.

C. S. Lewis in his fantasy about life after death, *The Great Divorce* wrote in the Preface the following reminder which may serve as a useful guide line to the reader of *Visions of the Spiritual World*: "I beg readers to remember that this is a fantasy. It has of course — or I intended it to have — a moral. But the transmortal conditions are solely an imaginative supposal: they are not even a guess or a speculation at what may actually await us. The last thing I wish is to arouse factual curiosity about the details of the afterworld."

C. S. Lewis was consciously creating a fantasy. Sundar Singh was not. However what he regarded as objective experiences may have been largely subjective. For this reason C. S. Lewis's directive is helpful.

Shortly after *Visions of the Spiritual World* was published he received a gift from the Swedenborg Society of several of Swedenborg's books. Despite his intention after visiting Swedenborg's tomb in Uppsala Cathedral of reading his works, Sundar had so far not found opportunity to do so. On reading them he discovered that his own visionary experiences coincided closely to those of Swedenborg. When A. J. Appasamy and Sundar met in 1928, Sundar was enthusiastic about the books and about his correspondence with John Goddard, Pastor Emeritus of the Swedenborg Church in Massachusetts, U.S.A. To Appasamy and in his letters to John Goddard, Sundar spoke of conversations he had had with Swedenborg in his visions.

This preoccupation with life after death must surely have received its impetus from Sundar's conviction that his own death was near at hand. In his tours abroad he had spoken little of his ecstatic experiences but he was prompted to record them believing that they were of value to others. He hoped that in sober print they might read less sensationally, making less appeal to mawkish curiosity, than would have been the case in a public address.

Believing that his time on earth was short, Sundar was also concerned with setting the record straight in another direction. In earlier years he had cared little what men had thought and said about him, and had appeared indifferent to the attacks on his integrity. His world tours in Europe and beyond had established his name internationally and during the 1920s the accusations against him had multiplied. Now, for the first time, Sundar himself took some part in refuting them. Realising that his books and his reputation would live on after his death, it is probable that he wanted to make them as effective a Christian witness as possible, and to this end he was concerned to answer his critics. What was the content of the case against him?

It was this, that some of the events in his life simply had not occurred in the way he had described. In particular the reliability of his assertions concerning the Maharishi of Kailash, his fast in Kajliban Forest and his miraculous escapes in Tibet were questioned. Some of his more vehement detractors even went so far as to believe him to be an out-and-out impostor, who had set out deliberately to deceive. Others were content to regard him as misguided, a man who was unable to distinguish between fact and fantasy.

His opponents lay in two camps, the Roman Catholics and in particular the Jesuits on the one hand and a Protestant faction on the other. Professor Friedrich Heiler in his Preface to the English edition of his book *The Gospel of Sadhu Sundar Singh* attributes their motives thus: "The Jesuits attack the Sadhu fearing lest the fact of his sanctity should weaken the claim of the Roman Church to be the only home of saints; Modernist Protestants, on the other hand, attack him because they fear that the Sadhu's 'miracles' may confirm the belief in the miracles of the Bible which they reject."

The Jesuit campaign against Sundar was led by Father H. Hosten, S.J., and that of the Protestant Modernists by Dr O. Pfister. The latter published a book *Die Legende Sundar Singhs* in which he argued that Sundar was a neurotic, unable to distinguish the real from the imagined, and whose relationship with Christ grew out of 'repressed infantile sex-complexes'.

Among those who rallied to his defence the most prominent was Professor Heiler whose aim in two books *Apostel oder Betruger?* (Apostle or Impostor?) and *Die Wahrheit Sundar Singhs* (The Truthfulness of Sundar Singh) was to answer the charges. In order to do this he gathered the testimonies of many people who had known Sundar. These ranged from Dr Fife, Headmaster of the Christian Boys' Boarding School at

Ludhiana who had befriended Sundar as a boy of fifteen, and Archbishop Nathan Soderblom whom Sundar had met in Uppsala in 1922.

Wherever possible he secured eye-witness reports of the incidents in dispute. Those who had known Sundar personally were convinced of his sincerity. The tribute of his friend, Thomas Riddle, in the *United Church Review* in August 1946, echoed the sentiments of those friends who had risen to his defence twenty years earlier:

> Many of us in India had long years of intimate contact with the Sadhu. It is not necessary for us to vindicate him. We know that he was a man of God. His personal spiritual life was a consistent witness to the fact that God was with him. God called him and used him in South India, and in Eastern and Western countries. We know that he did visit Tibet frequently, that he did fast to the limits of his strength near Dehra Dun; we know that his visions were no hallucinations but real unveilings of unseen mysteries. We know that he was sane, shrewd and level-headed in his judgment and was not dominated by gusts of sentiment. To him the presence of the living Lord was very real and the joy of that presence dwarfed every other human joy.

At the height of the debate Sundar himself wrote to Samuel Stokes asking him to vouch for him. Samuel Stokes had already received letters from people on both sides seeking his opinions and so he realised the significance of Sundar's request. It was however a request that put him in a dilemma. He did not in any way doubt Sundar's honesty, but he did have certain reservations about some of the incidents that were under scrutiny. It was Samuel Stokes who had been with him when Sundar almost drowned in an icy river. He had seen Sundar dragged from the water by a group of men. That these men were ordinary hillmen from the surrounding country he, Stokes, never for a moment doubted. Sundar however was convinced that they were angels sent by God. Stokes therefore answered Sundar's request in cautious terms. He wrote that he had never doubted that "to the best of your light and strength you have been trying to serve your Master". But he continued, "I hold you to be of a mystical temperament and think that you at times fail to distinguish, as clearly as might be, the borderline that runs between the subjective and objective in experience."

Samuel Stokes felt that he could not endorse the accuracy of all Sundar's recollections for the period they had worked together. It was obviously with a mounting dismay that Stokes had seen the controversy growing, and he believed that Sundar's friends were doing him a disservice in insisting on the literal truth of everything Sundar had said or written about his own experiences.

Sundar was disappointed in Stokes's attitude, but he attributed it to the latter's modernist approach to miracles. There was little that Sundar could do in his own defence and he was content to leave it to Professor Heiler and other influential friends.

When Bishop Appasamy visited him in 1928 Sundar gave the appearance of being quite unaffected by the storm that now surrounded his name, yet it is probable that he cared more deeply than he was prepared to admit.

The soaring snow-crowned peaks of the Himalayas that dominated the landscape to the north-west of Sabathu still beckoned Sundar towards Tibet just as they had twenty-three years earlier, when, as a boy of fifteen, he awaited his baptism in the peaceful atmosphere of the Sabathu Leper Hospital.

In the early summer of 1927 Sundar had set out once again

for Tibet but his impaired health was unable to withstand the strain. The Tibetans with whom he was travelling helped him to the nearest railway station and saw him safely on to a train back to Sabathu.

Two years later, in April 1929, Sundar determined to make another attempt. Sundar had never made elaborate preparations for his Tibetan journeys nor did he now. His correspondence was up to date, the papers and books in his room neat and tidy. One task remained. He sat at his desk and began a letter to Thomas Riddle, who was an executor of his will. Sundar had left all he possessed to the work of Christian education in India. He wrote:

> I'm leaving today for Tibet fully aware of the dangers and difficulties of the journey, but I must do my best to do my duty. I set no value on my own life as compared with the joy of finishing my course and fulfilling the commission I received from the Lord Jesus to attest the Gospel of the grace of God (Acts 20 : 24). I wanted to come to see you before leaving for Tibet, but I have received a letter from a trader to meet him at once on our way to Tibet. The route will be the same as that about which I told you last year. I hope to be back with one or two Tibetan Christians by the end of June. If anything happens I will send down Thapa to meet you, and if you do not hear anything from me, or about me, then please come to Sabathu in July in order to see to all my things in my house here.

Sundar sealed the letter. With characteristic absence of fuss and the minimum of baggage he was ready to leave. He had one call to make on his way through the town. He turned in through the gates of the Superintendent's house at the Leper Hospital and inquired for the Superintendent, G. H. Watson.

"The weather looks promising," he said. "I'm starting today for Tibet."

"You are not strong enough for such a journey," the Superindendent remonstrated. "Nor," he added, "have you done what I suggested. I told you to take a few long walks and get yourself fit."

Sundar smiled. "It's no good saying that. I am going. I have heard from the Tibetan traders. You won't persuade me to change my mind now. I have however one request to make. I am joining up with the Tibetans at Rishikesh. After that we shall take the road to Badrinath. I can travel to Rishikesh by train from Kalka. The road from Rishikesh to Badrinath is not too hard as we shall follow the way the pilgrims take on their way to the Hindu shrine at Badrinath. We shall leave the road before Badrinath, however, and make for the Niti Pass where we shall cross into Tibet. Could you look after my letters and answer the urgent ones? I hope to be back by the end of June."

"Of course I'll do that. I'll be only too glad."

The two men walked to the gates of the house where they were joined by Sannu Lal, an Indian preacher at the hospital. Sundar shook the Superintendent's hand and said good-bye.

"I'll walk part of the way with you, Sadhu," said Sannu Lal.

Perhaps, as he left Sabathu, Sundar turned back for a last look at the place he had known as home. It was always possible that he might never see it again, as he knew very well. A mile or so out of the town, Sannu Lal bade Sundar farewell and turned back.

The figure in the saffron robe made his way slowly and painfully along the road and disappeared into the distance. Sundar Singh had started on his last journey to Tibet. He was never to be seen again.

. . . . .

Thomas Riddle takes up the story at this point: "When June passed, and the middle of July, without any word having reached me, I felt that we owed it to the Indian Church that something should be done to get news of him. So at the end of July, Dr John C. Taylor of the Reformed Presbyterian Mission and I left Landour to follow his route up the hot Ganges Valley. We went back two hundred and twenty miles into the main range of the Himalayas, as far as the Tibetan border."

Riddle and Taylor constantly asked after him but always they drew a blank. They had high hopes of getting news at Srinagar where an old friend of Sundar's lived in a house no more than fifty yards off the road. If Sundar was travelling in the direction of Badrinath he would certainly have passed along that stretch of road. Surely he would have called in to say hello. They were disappointed. The old man had nothing to tell them.

As far as Joshimath the road was well defined but beyond this point their progress was impeded by rock falls. So frequently did they have to unload the mules and drag the luggage over the piles of rock, that they decided after resting at Tapoban to continue without the mules. Instead they hired three coolies and went on their way again. Their route was hazardous in the extreme. In his articles in 1946 for the *United Church Review*, and later in his book *The Vision and the Call*, Thomas Riddle describes a makeshift bridge they had to negotiate. "Across a span of fifty feet, with a roaring cataract below, three pine logs had been thrown, but it was a long span and the logs were neither supported below nor were their ends fixed. There was a foot of open space between each, and they rolled under our feet, and bobbed up and down deliriously, as with set teeth, we unsteadily picked our steps across. One of the hillmen coolies could not face it with a load, but crawled over on his hands and knees."

At another point in their journey they hired mountain ponies. "We started before daylight and soon reached a landslide on a wet and slippery hillside that had only a goat track across. I went forward to see if it was safe for the ponies to cross. There was a big drop below, and as I turned to get back I took hold of a stone in the rotten rock of the bank. It came away in my hand and that upset my sense of balance. Giddiness came on and I had an uncomfortable struggle to keep hold of myself, while with all sense of balance upset, I made myself go back to a wider bit of the road."

Hazards such as these, together with the news that there had been a severe outbreak of cholera amongst the pilgrims in May and June began to dash their hopes of finding Sundar alive. As they travelled farther along his intended route it became increasingly apparent that he had not preceded them. In remote villages beyond Joshimath the villagers, who saw so few travellers, were adamant that he had not passed their way.

It was no good. The search had to be abandoned. They had covered four hundred miles and for their pains had not uncovered a single scrap of information.

Mr Watson, the Hospital Superintendent at Sabathu, entrusted with Sundar's correspondence, sent out a circular letter to his friends on 3rd September 1929, which was Sundar's fortieth birthday. He told them of the fruitless search and ended his letter thus:

> His last and, in my opinion, his best book, published only this year, viz *With and Without Christ*, enables us to believe that if he has come to the end of his earthly journey he is now realising the 'Living Presence of Christ' more fully than ever before . . . hence we can but thank God for the joyful

state of our brother Sadhu Sundar Singh, and look forward to the happy reunion in the Lord's presence also.

There the matter rests. What befell Sundar on his final journey into Tibet remains a mystery to this day, although there have been many speculations. His own failing health, the rampant cholera or the dangerous conditions of the journey may well have caused his death even before he reached Tibet with its own particular risks. The news broke upon the world in the autumn of 1929 that Sundar Singh was missing and in all probability had died.

This notice appeared in *The Times* for 28th April, 1933:

> The probate of Sadhu Sundar Singh's Will has been granted in India as a consequence of the official presumption of his death by the Government of India on the ground that there has been no news of him since 1929, when he visited Tibet.

Had he died? There were those who would not give up hope, who put forward other theories to account for his disappearance. Some held the view that he had chosen to spend the remainder of his life on earth in meditation and like the Maharishi of Kailash had withdrawn from human company to the solitude of a remote mountain cave. In fact a plausible case for such a view can be made. Sundar might have felt that, in light of his failing health, the most valuable service he could perform was prayer and prayer alone, and that this, henceforth, should occupy him totally. Such a desire might have been reinforced almost unconsciously by an urge to get away from the wearisome controversy about his own integrity. A yearning for solitude in the latter years of life was not unusual in India, and it was a yearning firmly rooted in centuries of religious culture.

Yet it would not have been in his character deliberately to cause his friends such distress, or deliberately to mislead them. All his letters indicated that it was his intention to return though he recognised a strong possibility that he would not. The care with which he had put his affairs in order in case he did not come back indicate exactly how strong he felt that possibility to be.

As a young man he had hoped that his span of life might equal Our Lord's, and when his thirty-third year came and went, friends noticed that he was saddened that this was not to be. To die in the active service of his Master was his desire. To set out for Tibet in his frail condition was a reckless act. In choosing to go to Tibet it was as if he gathered up his last reserves of strength to make one final sacrifice of love and devotion for his Lord.

> Ready for all thy perfect will,
>   My acts of faith and love repeat,
> Till death thy endless mercies seal,
>   And make my sacrifice complete.
>
> (Charles Wesley, 1707–88).

Postscript

THIS IS THE brief record of his life. What difference has it made that this young Indian lived and died? What is it to us fifty years on?

His personal ministry brought Christ alive to thousands. In his writings his influence on individuals continues today.

However his life has a timeless importance as relevant now as it was then. For in that life we are aware of one who was a true mediator. He was the 'bridge' that spanned apparently divergent points of view. In a world that is hedged about with walls and frontiers he stands out as one who crosses the barriers. In him we see a positive, hard-won union, not a negative compromise between that which separates man from man and one set of values from another. He was in so many ways a bridge-builder.

We have already seen how Sundar Singh held a firm and steady balance between the life of an active evangelist and the interior life of prayer. This living out of the Christian ideal has a particular relevance for Western Christianity which, as Evelyn Underhill points out, is characterised by a "Western emphasis on doing and Western contempt for being". In *The Life of the Spirit and the Life of Today* (Methuen & Co. Ltd. 1922) she wrote:

> Our spiritual life today, such as it is, tends above all to express itself in social activities. Teacher after teacher comes forward to plume himself on the fact that Christianity is now taking a 'social form'; that love of our neighbour is not so much the corollary as the equivalent of the love of God, and so forth . . . Yet is there in this state of things nothing but

> food for congratulation? Is such a view complete? Is nothing left out? Have we not lost the wonder and poetry of the forest in our diligent cultivation of the economically valuable trees; and shall we ever see life truly until we see it with the poet's eyes? There is so much meritorious working and willing; and so little time left for quiet love.

The trend continues today and modern Christians find Evelyn Underhill's warning and Sundar Singh's example especially relevant.

It was the burden of Sundar's message on his visits to Europe and America. To the undergraduates at Oxford, to the young people at Silver Bay in the United States, to the Swiss pastors his counsel was the same: Pray! Do not cut yourselves adrift from the source of life. He was convinced that the Christians of the West had for too long set too little store by the spiritual dimension. He found, and would find today, that for millions there is only one 'real' dimension—the here and now world of sight, sound and touch, the world perceived by physical senses. He found, and would find, only a limited acknowledgment of any other world, the world which we glimpse through a glass darkly.

Sundar's spiritual awareness was instinctive because he was an Indian and also because of his upbringing. His mother nurtured the gift in him. Charles Andrews described the Indian outlook as 'medieval'. There is a similarity between the India of Sundar's day and the Europe of the Middle Ages in their easy acceptance of the supernatural.

This is the backdrop against which we should view the miracles, the escapes and the visions. This is not to say that the modern reader should suspend his critical faculties, for this perhaps is the capacity that the West can offer to the rest of the world. We must indeed ask the question formulated by

Professor Leonard Hodgson in his book *For Faith and Freedom* (Oxford 1956): "What must the truth be, and have been, if it appeared like that to men who thought and wrote as they did?" Professor Hodgson offered this question as a guideline to the student of the New Testament—a plea that Biblical texts should be studied bearing in mind the background, character and thought-processes of those who wrote them and those for whom they were written. Should not we likewise have regard for the culture and thought forms of Sundar's day when reflecting upon the more inexplicable and incongruous aspects of his life?

Sundar, embodying the union of the life of active evangelism and the hidden life of prayer, was thus bridging another gap, the chasm between Eastern and Western religious insights. Not only was he reminding the West of the centrality of the spiritual life, but also he put before the East the claims of human compassion for one's neighbour. Social conscience has not featured conspicuously in the East partly on account of an indifference to man's physical well-being. Sundar who, as a boy, took money from his father to buy a blanket for a destitute woman, who, as a man, nursed the lepers at Sabathu Hospital and who risked his own life to carry to safety the man found unconscious in the snow, was advocating the better way of the Samaritan.

In his relationship with the Indian Church Sundar Singh stands out again as one who unifies. For historical reasons the Indian Church, particularly in the North, was an importation from abroad. English hymns, Victorian piety—these were the outward symbols of the captivity of the Indian Church. It was the custom for Indians, on embracing the Christian faith, to adopt European dress, thus seeming to set themselves apart from their fellow countrymen.

Sundar showed the Church that pride in one's Indian heritage could be combined with Christianity. Indian converts could be truly Indian and truly Christian.

The New Testament was Sundar's constant inspiration. The background of his early family life meant that he had little contact with institutional Christianity. He came to his faith through opening his mind to the pages of the New Testament. The Gospels themselves influenced him more powerfully than the witness of any church community or the witness of individual believers. His faith was fresh and it was never to lose its freshness, ever preserved by his devotion to the person of Christ through the power of the Holy Spirit.

For the Indian Church in need of an indigenous ideal, the appearance of Sundar Singh on the scene was vastly important.

His way of life as a sadhu was wholly authentic. His method of teaching by parable paralleled the Hindu system of analogy as a method of religious instruction. The stress he placed on silence and meditation in a believer's life was in complete accord with the Indian outlook. He never claimed that his way was the *only* way, but that the Indian Christian could find, without looking outside his own culture, every necessary means of expressing his Christian commitment.

The Indian Church in the early part of this century must be seen against the background of the national movement towards independence, a movement which naturally and rightly encouraged Indians to be loyal to their own heritage. The barriers between the denominations were beginning to fall, resulting in a more flexible attitude in matters of doctrine. Side by side with this movement was a shift in the theological climate which now began to encourage the study of Comparative Religion. Among Indian Christians there was a revival of interest in Hinduism. Need Christianity and Hinduism be mutually exclusive? For example, J. N. Farquhar in *The Crown of Hinduism* (Oxford

1913) saw an *evolutionary* connection between Hinduism and Christianity as of lower to higher, so that what is only foreshadowed in Hinduism is fulfilled and perfected in Christianity. He believed that Christ's declaration, "I came not to destroy but to fulfil," should be applied not only in relation to Judaism but also to Hinduism and other world religions.

So far the efforts to achieve a synthesis between the two had been muddled and incomplete. Sundar had little time for academic theological arguments. They were dry bones for him. His theology (he would never have used the term!) was spontaneous and instinctive, nourished by his relationship with Jesus Christ. He drew on this inexhaustible spring for teaching, his method, like that of Jesus, being mainly by simple parables drawn from nature. Although he did not aim for a logical system of belief, his parables taken as a whole reveal a natural and unconstrained coherence, with Christ always at their heart.

His attitude towards his own suffering reveals this Christ-centredness and is also a development or fulfilment of Hindu asceticism. Robin Boyd in *An Introduction to Indian Christian Theology* (The Christian Literature Society, Madras 1969) wrote:

> His life was completely selfless and he frequently underwent severe hardship, but his asceticism was not the rigid asceticism of *hatha yoga*, which he rejected. His aim was rather to bear witness, through suffering gladly accepted, to Christ's love and grace, and he speaks often of the joy of suffering, of the peace of the Christian way, and the life of union with Christ as 'Heaven upon Earth'. He vividly illustrates the nature of suffering by telling a story of a doctor striking a weakly new-born baby in order to make it cry and so begin to breathe.

Thus Sundar accepted suffering in a positive way, but never did he seek it or inflict it upon himself for the alleged refinement of his soul.

This belief that all things work together for good to those who love God was the mainspring of a steadfast sense of peace and awareness of Christ's presence. This awareness came to him most strongly in extremes of hardship. Turned out of his father's home into the cold night he knew 'his first night in heaven'. Sick with fever he said to Samuel Stokes, "How sweet it is to suffer for His sake!" Of his treatment in the prison at Ilam, he wrote, "For two or three hours I felt my sufferings very much indeed but afterwards my Lord by His Holy Presence turned my prison into paradise."

In *Reality and Religion* Sundar gives another parable on the nature of suffering in the chapter 'The Cross': "Diamonds do not dazzle with beauty unless they are cut. When cut, the rays of the sun fall on them and make them shine with wonderful colours. So when we are cut by the cross we shall shine as jewels in the Kingdom of God."

Sundar's influence upon Indian theology is to be seen in the work of theologians like his friend Aiyadurai Jesudasen Appasamy. Indeed Robin Boyd goes so far as to suggest, "It might even prove ultimately that in the history of the Indian Church and its thought Sundar Singh was actually more important for his theology and its method than for his ascetic way of life and his success as an evangelist."

There are still many hindrances which slow down the Indian Church from evolving her own identity. She has yet to achieve total liberation from what C. F. Andrews called the 'Western captivity' of the Indian Church. However the Church of South India and the Church of North India are in themselves repudiations of those historical divisions once sadly imported from the West. There is also the heartening and ongoing desire to implement the original aim of the Church of South India as expressed in her Constitution, "to conserve all that is of spiritual value in its Indian heritage, to express under Indian conditions and in Indian forms the spirit, the thought and the life of the Church universal." How Sundar Singh would have approved of that!

The simplicity of his life and thought, so close in tone and spirit to the pages of the New Testament bridges another gap, namely the two thousand years which separates the birth of Christianity from our present day. It is not only the Indian Church that needs to look beneath the veil of Western church history and Western culture. Western Christians have the same need.

Professor Friedrich Heiler in *The Gospel of Sadhu Sundar Singh* wrote: "The whole history of Western Christianity presents the spectacle of an ever-renewed drift away from the centre, a continual flight to the circumference . . . Again and again it has mistaken the rind for the kernel, the rays of sunshine for the light itself." When we read Sundar Singh's life, centuries of church history seem to drop away. In his deep personal attachment to Christ, he was so close to the source of the Gospel and a most striking feature of his faith is its freshness.

In assessing Sundar's contribution to the witness of the Church in this century Professor Heiler wrote this moving passage:

> . . . it is undeniable that Sundar Singh is an evangelist both to the East and to the West. He has, in fact, a double message: for India, that in spite of much precious wealth she has not yet found the pearl of great price, the Gospel pearl; and for the Christian West, that she indeed possesses this precious pearl, but that it has been almost lost amidst

the heap of accumulations made by theology, Church, and culture.

One of these 'accumulations' was of course the division of Christ's body into denominations. Perhaps Sundar's kinship with the New Testament age is most clearly expressed in his detachment from a narrow denominational loyalty. He regarded his membership of the Church of England as a matter of no great consequence, of no greater significance in the ultimate order of things than the fact that he was born in 1889, that his birthplace was Rampur, or that he preferred mountains to the plains.

This ecumenism meant that he was unconsciously both Catholic and Protestant. Here too we see him as a mediator. His mysticism, his ready acceptance of the miraculous, his wandering sadhu life-style reminiscent of the mendicant friars of the Middle Ages, all have their counterparts in Catholicism. Yet his devotion to Scripture, his belief in personal conversion and his disregard for the authority of the institutional Church are all redolent of Protestantism. This was not a deliberate choosing of a little from here and a little from there in the hope of attaining an accepable synthesis, since Sundar was, first and foremost, true to his own conscience. His Christian faith was derived from the New Testament and thus had its roots in an age when the labels 'Catholic' and 'Protestant' were irrelevant.

Thus we see him as the bridge-builder, a man who strove to close the gaps between East and West, between Christian and Hindu, between the Church of the Acts of the Apostles and the church of the twentieth century, between the physical world and the spiritual world and between varying Christian traditions.

Throughout a courageous life he held on to that great truth which Saint Paul sought to convey to the Galatians:

"There is no such thing
as Jew and Greek, slave
and freeman, male and
female; for you are all
one person in Christ
Jesus." (Galatians, Chapter 3, v. 28 NEB).